MW01609977

# The Renewal of Independence

## *The Nation's Renewed Dependence on Independence*

J. Caroline DeBerry

HESTER PUBLICATIONS

Photography by J. Caroline DeBerry

Edited by Dr. Margaret Payne

Published by Hester Publications
Henderson, Tennessee

www.hesterpublications.com

*Dedicated to*
*President George W. Bush*
*and*
*First Lady Laura Bush*

# CONTENTS

*Prologue*   **1**

## *PART I* — DEFINITION OF INDEPENDENCE

### ONE
*Independence: A Legacy to Defend*   **5**

### TWO
*Independence: In Their Own Words*   **11**

### THREE
*Independence: A Living Legacy*   **17**

### FOUR
*Independence: A Responsibility to Respect*   **23**

## *PART II* — LAWS OF INDEPENDENCE

### FIVE
*The U.S. Constitution Construed*   **29**

### SIX
*Clauses for Concern*   **33**

### SEVEN
*Malleable Meanings*   **43**

EIGHT

*The Bailout Bill: Bailing Out on the American People* **49**

NINE

*Health Care Reform: A Diagnosis* **71**

*PART III* — **DEFENSE OF INDEPENDENCE**

TEN

*Take Note of the Vote* **87**

ELEVEN

*Run for the Right Reasons* **93**

TWELVE

*Let Someone Else Do It* **101**

THIRTEEN

*Special Considerations for College Students* **109**

*Conclusion*:

**INHERITANCE OF INDEPENDENCE** **113**

*Appendix* **117**

*Acknowledgements* **121**

*Notes* **123**

# *Prologue*

On August 25, 2009, Massachusetts's U.S. Senator Ted Kennedy—the brother of assassinated U.S. President John F. Kennedy and a key power player in United States politics and government—died of brain cancer. A well-known advocate of healthcare reform, Senator Kennedy left behind a legacy of leadership and determination to promote ideals of the Democratic Party. It was expected by the nation that this leader's now empty seat would be filled in the Massachusetts special election by a fellow Democrat, who would continue the agendas of his or her predecessor. Yet, everyone underestimated the power of independents. Everyone underestimated the power of Massachusetts citizens' innate or inherited desire for independence.

On January 19, 2010, the Republican candidate Scott Brown stunned the nation by taking Kennedy's Senate seat. The keys to his victory appeared to be the independent voters of Massachusetts.[1] Yet, independent voters were considered significantly influential in the outcome of the 2008 presidential campaign.[2] How such an unbelievable turn in events could happen was hard to explain by the media and Democrats, especially when their president Barack Obama was believed to carry so much tout and public adoration. Yet, the common citizen—especially the Massachusetts citizen—understood the unexpected uprising of independent voters. Theirs is the heritage of the foundation of this nation; they, as do all U.S. citizens, hunger for the freedom—the independence—that characterizes the United States of America as a unique country in history…the liberty for which much blood has been shed over the course of centuries.

1

# PART I:
## THE DEFINITION OF INDEPENDENCE

# 1

## INDEPENDENCE: A LEGACY TO DEFEND

Tomahawks wielded, men sneaked aboard ships anchored in the Boston dock. Anyone noticing many of the men would have assumed they were Indians, as the men had planned with their disguises. The target of their tomahawks was not other men; it was boxes of tea. On December 16, 1773, in the event to become known as the Boston Tea Party, a group of colonists dumped three ships' cargo of tea into the Boston Harbor to prevent the British from shooting cannon balls into the town the next morning, according to an eyewitness named George Hewes.[3] This was one of many incidents which sounded the drum roll for the War for Independence in 1776.

Less than three years later, the room seemed heavy with the solemnity of the moment. Fifty-five men knew that death was a risk they were undertaking by participating in the momentous occasion on July 4, 1776.[4] One by one, eventually fifty-six men in all took ink and a quill and assigned their "John Hancocks"—their signatures—onto a piece of paper. Yet, this piece of paper would become more than paper. It would become a revered document that would change the world. It put into words—into pen and ink—the desires of millions of people from the past, the present, and the future. The Declaration of Independence was a revolution in and of itself, representing the extraordinary courage, confidence, and determination of its signers and their constituents—British colonists, who had just become new citizens of the United States of America.

These signers are rightly hallowed in history as men of incredible strength and foresight. They changed the course of history—by simply using ink and pen to express their opinions and convictions. They were to take up their arms and fight, but the Declaration of Independence itself dramatically changed the world's understanding of independence and freedom. Often, it seems Americans lose sight of this heritage—particularly that these men were mere men. They themselves were ordinary men, but what made these signers of the Declaration of Independence extraordinary was their decision to act, lead, and exert their rights as humans. Such is a decision—an opportunity—available to every citizen of the United States. That is the freedom in which each signer believed as he took the quill. That is the legacy they established for future generations.

Acknowledging the signers' ordinary nature, it is still difficult to grasp the extent of this truth. A brief look at the lives of a few signers of the Declaration of Independence, utilizing the following information provided by the Independence Hall Association, can help in this effort to recognize these men's common backgrounds.[5]

George Read of Delaware was a renown lawyer, active in politics and government as an attorney general; this signer and member of the Continental Congress, born on a farm in Maryland, became the chief justice of Delaware in 1782 and served in that office for sixteen years.

Caesar Rodney of Delaware, also born on a farm, only possessed an informal education and suffered the loss of his father at age seventeen. Yet, he became a great civil servant through his official capacities, beginning at age twenty-two as Kent County's High Sheriff.

George Ross of Pennsylvania was one of many children in his family and "received a sound classical education at home"—which he put to use by teaching himself law and becoming a vocal advocate of the colonies and their rights.

Benjamin Rush of Pennsylvania lost his father at age six, but thanks to the direction of his mother, he was provided excellent guidance and a formal education through the efforts of his uncle and others. As a physician, Rush looked to the needs of those in poverty and became the first to publish a chemistry textbook in America.

James Smith of Pennsylvania became an immigrant from Ireland at age ten or twelve. Educated by a Pennsylvania minister and his brother (who was a lawyer), Smith had limited opportunity to serve the public as a lawyer and subsequently worked primarily as a surveyor, until he moved to a larger town. He authored a paper encouraging colonists to boycott British products and led volunteer militia in the American Revolution.

George Taylor of Pennsylvania was too an Irish immigrant; he first came to the colonies in his early twenties. Despite his lack of passion for politics and his occupations in iron production, he helped change the course of history through his signature on the Declaration of Independence and other political efforts prior to and following the signing of the Declaration.

James Wilson of Pennsylvania never earned a college degree, despite study at multiple Scottish universities. After immigrating to America from Scotland in his twenties, Wilson taught at Philadelphia College, became a lawyer (eventually taking on cases from eight different nearby counties), and purchased a farm. His political career was sparked when his publication advocating colonies' rights was noted by the

Continental Congress.

Edward Rutledge of South Carolina was born into aristocracy in Charleston; with this privileged beginning, Rutledge took advantage of his opportunity as a wealthy colonist and became a great leader in politics through his study of law, attendance in Congress, and his military service.

Roger Sherman of Connecticut spent his childhood years in a frontier town. Yet, his limited surroundings did not prevent his learning. Sherman obtained an education using his father's library, the town's grammar school (built when he was approximately thirteen years old), and the parish minister (a Harvard graduate). Beginning his career in public service as a surveyor, Sherman gradually came to guide the public in higher and higher capacities (in addition to establishing with his brother the first store in his hometown).

William Williams of Connecticut appears to have spent every minute of his life educating himself, working, or serving the public through government—including his service as the town clerk in Lebanon for forty-four years and as a legislator for almost forty years.

Richard Stockton of New Jersey received an excellent education, graduating from the College of New Jersey—the institution now known as Princeton University. Politics did not greatly interest Stockton, though he was a lawyer; yet, he was appointed to the New Jersey Supreme Court and was later chosen to serve as a delegate to the Continental Congress. According to historical reports, Stockton was not a man to be told what to do or how to think, at least in the matters of colonial independence; he refused to vote for independence until he listened to "the arguments on either side of the issue." Thanks to his support of the War for Independence and British retaliation, Stockton died a poor man but an independent patriot.

Matthew Thornton of New Hampshire rose to the position of surgeon for the troops of New Hampshire from his humble beginning as an Irish immigrant at age three. Thornton even became the author of New Hampshire's first state constitution—the first state constitution to be written "after the start of hostilities with Britain."

William Whipple of New Hampshire attended a "common school," but as a teenager, became a seaman. His involvement in the government began shortly after he and his brother became partners as merchants in Portsmouth, eventually rising to the position of associate judge for the New Hampshire Superior Court.

George Walton of Georgia became an orphan at an early age; he became a carpenter, at the direction of his uncle—who had adopted him following his parents' death. History has left us little record of his younger years; but his study of law, beginning in 1769, resulted in a long involvement in government and politics—becoming a prisoner of war in the War for Independence, governor of Georgia (briefly two different times), U.S. Senator, and other leadership positions.

The stories of these famous signers of the Declaration of Independence inspire people from all walks of life to realize the opportunities available to them to exercise and defend their rights as independent, free citizens of the United States of America—a country established with the stroke of a pen by fifty-six great, but ordinary, men.

# 2

## INDEPENDENCE: IN THEIR OWN WORDS

The War for Independence was undoubtedly one of history's greatest efforts made by humankind in assertion of the concept of freedom and individual rights and liberties. What was it like to live in that time period? What was it like to be amongst the writings or even the actual leaders of that era? Imagination can conceive of the great impact of the actual words of these extraordinary leaders with ordinary backgrounds...

A blacksmith smiled as he walked into the store. It was that time of year again. He picked up a copy of the latest *Poor Richard's Almanack*; his friend Benjamin Franklin did an excellent job with these. The blacksmith and his father had been buying the little pamphlets ever since he could remember. Towards the end of the 1758 pamphlet, he read, "And now to conclude, *Experience keeps a dear School, but fools will learn in no other, and scarce in that*; for it is true, *we may give Advice, but we cannot give Conduct,* as *Poor Richard* says: However, remember this, *They that won't be counseled, can't be helped,* as *Poor Richard* says: And farther, That *if you will not hear Reason, she'll surely rap your Knuckles.*"[6] The blacksmith hoped his young son William would live according such wisdom as he grew into a man.

Almost twenty years later, a blacksmith named William walked into a store and purchased the latest, highly popular publication. His father, also a blacksmith, had instilled in him the value of learning from the wisdom of others. As he walked out with the small book, *Common Sense* by Thomas Paine, he flipped through the pages. A passage caught his eyes: "Ye that oppose independence now, ye know not what ye do; ye are opening a door to eternal tyranny, by keeping vacant the seat of government."[7] It was a thought provoking, inspiring statement.

Only months later, William was relieved his time to serve was almost up. It was only day since prior to the crossing of the Delaware River, his officer read portions of Thomas Paine's *The American Crisis*.[8] He believed in the cause. He believed in freedom—for his wife, children, and someday hopefully their children…his grandchildren. He felt serving under George Washington was an honor, but he was exhausted and missed his family. Many said he had served his time and fulfilled any duty he had; a few others, such as distant family in Britain, said it was a wasted effort. William listened as General Washington spoke to the troops:

> My brave fellows, … You have done all I have asked you to do and more than could be reasonably expected. But your country is at stake; your wives, your houses, and all that you hold dear. You have worn yourself out with fatigues and hardships but we know not how to spare you. If you will consent to stay but one month longer you will render that service to the cause of liberty and to your country which you probably never can do under any other circumstances. The present is emphatically the

crisis which is to decide our destiny.[9]

William looked around at his comrades. He knew what he would do. He wanted independence, regardless of what others said.

A lady sighed as she remembered her father William; she missed him each day. She picked up a book, published last year, 1792; there was one sentence in it she loved. In the book, the author had written, "Independence I have long considered as the grand blessing of life, the basis of every virtue...."[10] Each time William's daughter read the sentence she reflected on her father's stories of serving as a soldier in the great War of Independence.

About four years later, on September 26, William's daughter picked up the day's newspaper. The word "independence" caught her eye on the front page of *The Connecticut Courage*. She smiled as she read a couple of sentences:

> The unity of government which constitutes you one people, is also now dear to you. It is justly so; for it is a main pillar in the edifice of your real independence, the support of your tranquility at home, your peace abroad; of your safety: of your prosperity; of that very Liberty which you so highly prize.[11]

William's daughter sighed as she sat to finish reading the farewell address of her father's general during the War of Independence and her nation's first President—George Washington.

Even without imagining the effects of leaders' writings on fictional characters, history illustrates the unwavering determination of this nation's Founding Fathers and the nation's early patriots. Such conviction is demonstrated in the words of a letter written in 1778 to a mother; the letter explained the author's driving conviction:

> ...While my country calls for the exertion of that little share of abilities which it has pleased God to bestow on me, I hold it my indispensable duty to give myself to her. I know that for such sentiments, which are not fashionable among the folks you see, I am called a rebel.[12]

The son and author of the letter was Gouverneur Morris. His writings record that he visited troops at Valley Forge during that horrendous winter of 1777-78; there he saw courageous troops shivering in the cold—in need of physical and moral support.[13] Likely, these images helped to strengthen Gouverneur Morris's passion for freedom and country. Only years later, he would help form and would sign into law the Supreme Law of the Land—the Constitution of the United States.

In June of 1796, (while running for the presidency as a Democratic-Republican[14]) in a personal letter from one great leader to another, Thomas Jefferson expressed to George Washington his dedication to the value which had resulted in the great Declaration of Independence twenty years before. "But when urged by others, I have never conceived that having been in public life requires me to belie my sentiments, or even to conceal them. When I am led by conversation to express them, I do it with the same independence here which I have practiced everywhere, and which is inseparable from my nature."[15]

The dedication to authoring law which would ensure freedom for all inspired one Illinois man, not quite thirty years old. Speaking to the Young Men's Lyceum of Springfield, Illinois, in 1837, this man referred to the Founding Fathers:

> As the patriots of seventy-six did to the support of the Declaration of Independence, so to the support of the Constitution and laws let every American pledge his life, his property, and his sacred honor—let every man remember that to violate the law is to trample on the blood of his father, to tear the charter of his own and his children's liberty. Let reverence for the laws be breathed by every American mother to the lisping babe that prattles on her lap; let it be taught in schools, in seminaries, and in colleges; let it be written in primers, spelling-books, and in almanacs; let it be preached from the pulpit, proclaimed in legislative halls, and enforced in courts of justice.[16]

The speaker was none other than Abraham Lincoln—who would, despite political odds, strive to use law (the Emancipation Proclamation) to grant independence to slaves and free the nation from that bondage.

A leader amongst African Americans, Booker T. Washington understood independence from a different perspective than the majority of his fellow citizens. Even from a practical standpoint, he understood concepts that the Founding Fathers comprehended but many of Booker T. Washington's contemporaries took for granted. Washington struggled to help fellow freed slaves live their independence—realizing that without economic independence, they truly had nothing. He wrote in *An Autobiography: The Story of My Life and Work*, "Independence and debt cannot long keep company."[17]

Many great voices have urged fellow men and women to fight for freedom. Their words of wisdom have inspired generation upon generation, each voice expressing the meaning of that great concept of independence with his or her own unique perspective. Behind each of those great voices was an ordinary person. It was their fearless, inspiring calls to action and decisive efforts which made them extraordinary leaders—who would define and depict true independence for all people of all ages and generations.

# 3

## INDEPENDENCE: A LIVING LEGACY

During the years leading up to the Revolutionary War, the leaders of the time believed in the idea of freedom in a broad, permanent sense that the world had never yet seen. These men and women believed in a reality of freedom for all ensured by a government limited by the people whom they represented—a reality that they knew was possible but had never yet been truly accomplished. They heeded the warnings of history and grasped the surety of their purpose, never losing sight of their ultimate goal—even years before the Declaration of Independence was signed. The following quotations from the book of various writings by the men of the Continental Congress—*Letters of Members of the Continental Congress*[18]—reveal these leaders' dogged determination to ensure a life of freedom for posterity.

In May 1776, Elbridge Gerry best summarized the state of the people and the government by saying, "... I think the Colonies cannot long remain an independent depending People...." Colonel Bland in September 1774 concisely voiced the true issue at hand by saying, "The question is, whether the rights and liberties of America shall be contended for, or given up to arbitrary power."

In September 1774, James Duane asserted the importance

of representative government, rather than tyranny:

> Every Institution, legislative and Judicial, essential to the Exercise and Enjoyment of these Rights and priviledges [sic] in constitutional security were equally their Birth right and inalienable Inheritance. They coud [sic] not be withheld but by lawless oppression, and by lawless oppression only can they be violated.
>
> ... These respective Rights cannot be altered or abridged by any other Authority than that of their respective Legislatures.

Almost three weeks later, Joseph Galloway expressed words which solidified his colleague's:

> ... It is most evident, upon a due consideration of it, that the rights of America would have been fully restored, and her freedom effectually secured by it. For under it no law can be binding on America, to which the people, by their Representatives, have not previously given their consent: this is the essence of liberty, and what more would her people desire?

A true believer in the cause, Joseph Galloway described himself, saying, "I am as much a friend of liberty as exists; and no man shall go further in point of fortune, or in point of blood, than the man who now addresses you."

Words of inspiration to one another and fellow colonists empowered them to prepare for the struggle ahead. President of the Continental Congress John Hancock exclaimed, on November 30, 1775:

> You have hitherto risen superior to a Thousand Difficulties

in giving Freedom to a great and an oppressed People. ... Proceed therefore, and let the Footsteps of Victory open a Way for Blessings of Liberty, and the Happiness of well-ordered Government to visit that extensive Dominion. ... Reflect, Sir, that the Happiness, or Misery, of Millions yet unborn, is now to be determined; and remember that you will receive an honourable [sic] Compensation for all your Fatigues, in being able to leave the Memory of illustrious Actions, attended by the Gratitude of a great and free People, as a fair, a splendid, and a valuable Inheritance, to your Posterity.

Almost a year later, John Hancock rallied his New Hampshire audience with these words:

They are called upon to say, whether they will live Slaves, or die Freemen—they are requested to step forth in Defence [sic] of their Wives, their Children, and Liberty, and every Thing they hold dear. The Cause is certainly a most glorious one, and I trust every Man in the Colony of New Hampshire is determined to see it gloriously ended, or perish in the Ruins of it.

Long before the end of the struggle—the ultimate victory—two men, John Sullivan and John Langdon, depicted the state of unity of the colonists on June 20, 1775: "It is impossible to conceive of a greater unanimity in the Colonies, than that which at present subsists, one and all being Determined to defend our Rights to the last."

By May 1776, Oliver Olcott predicted or planned for the future, stating:

A Revolution in Goverment [sic], you will perceive, is about to take Effect. May God Grant a happy Establishment of it, and secuerety [sic] to the Rights of the Rights of the People. If this Recommendation takes effect which undouptedly [sic] it will, There will be an instance Real not implied or Ideal of a Goverment [sic] founded in Compacet [sic] Express and Clear Made in its Principles by the People at large.

Future president of the United States John Adams indicated his resolve to never lose sight of freedom when he said, in the summer of 1775, "... We shall have Occasion for all our Wit Vigilance and Virtue to avoid being deceived, wheedled threatened or bribed out of our Freedom" (152). The drum roll of freedom filled the air, as July 4, 1776, approached. In June of 1776, Adams pronounced, "It is now universally acknowledged that we are and must be independent." Like the final screw put into place before a ship sets sail, on July 1, 1776, John Adams reported:

A declaration that these colonies are free and independent States, had been reported by a committee appointed some weeks ago for that purpose, and this day or to-morrow is to determine its fate. May Heaven prosper the new-born republic, and make it more glorious than any former republics have been!

Despite the hardships, the discouraging moments, the ridicule, and the periods of hopelessness, the leaders of the American Revolution never surrendered. They never capitulated to "arbitrary power"—tyranny or the absence of freedom—forsaking all odds. With every bullet, every speech, every article, and every sacrifice—they fought for what they viewed as their purpose...the purpose of establishing a system of government which would provide freedom for all.

Even as early as October 1774, freedom was a treasure to

many, as explained by John Dickinson, when he proclaimed, "A determined and unanimous resolution animates this Continent, firmly and faithfully to support the common cause to the utmost extremity, in this great struggle for the blessing of liberty—a blessing that alone can render life worth holding."

The profits of their labors and struggles remain with us today, as do their words. Over two hundred years have come and gone, but these great human leaders' words should spark a fire—a life—into the concept of freedom. Through their words and their victories, every citizen of the United States of America possesses a living legacy. May the United States forever honor and follow the words of James Duane, who said in May 1775:

On our side we tremble for the dearest and most inestimable of all earthly blessings, our liberty and for those rights and that most excellent constitution and free government, which (resources) were procured by the blood and handed down to us by the wisdom and the bravery of our renowned ancestors.

# 4

## INDEPENDENCE:

## A RESPONSIBILITY TO RESPECT

Independence has many aspects and facets but is, at the core, freedom—the ability to act freely without restraint by or dependence upon others. A word often used to define independence is self-sufficiency. Independence in the context of freedom from governmental intervention or restriction certainly has an element of self-sufficiency. Such is evidenced by the words of President John F. Kennedy—words that have inspired millions for decades: "And so, my fellow Americans: Ask not what your country can do for you—ask what you can do for your country."[19]

One can compare independence to money. Money is worthless, unless it is used—through investing, saving, or spending. So independence is worthless to an individual if he or she does not use it. What is the point of having the right to vote—if a citizen never votes? "My vote doesn't count; it can't make that much of a difference" are excuses used by many non-voters. But what if all citizens were to cease to vote? Besides, the truth of the matter is—every vote does count, as discussed in a later chapter.

What is the value in having the right and freedom to speak

out—to voice concerns and beliefs—if one does not ever utilize this liberty? Voting is not the only method of speaking out. Why did so many shed their blood that others would have the opportunity to listen to the news freely and educate themselves—if no one cares who wins an election or what their representatives in D.C. or at the city council do?

It begins with each citizen. It begins with the individual. If almost each individual were to assume his or her neighbor will be the activist and will be the one who votes, then the fate of the nation will rest in the hands of very few—despite the desperate, dedicated work and sacrifice of those gone on before to provide the privilege of independence to every citizen of the United States. Is such a state true independence and freedom for all?

Apathy is a killer. If a fire begins in the basement, obviously everyone in the house will either evacuate or try to squelch the fire. If the occupants just ignore the fire or assume someone else will take care of it, the consequences will likely be deadly.

Apathy is also similar to cancer; it spreads. If one person does not seem to care about a problem, it will be easier for the next person to ignore the problem too. If a teacher does not have a passion or sincere appreciation for the history of the United States, he or she will teach the students to see the nation's history as merely material to learn for the next test—rather than as the heritage it truly is.

If apathy becomes too prevalent among citizens of the United States, independence will be lost. Independence requires action and defense on the part of whomever possesses it. That is part of self-sufficiency. That is the responsibility which comes with this freedom—just as frugal usage of money is a responsibility of owning it.

Another significant component of self-sufficiency is thinking for oneself. In a free nation such as the United

States, individuals have had the liberty to put their brilliance into action—through innovations which have led to efficient production methods, computers, iPhones, electronic entertainment (such as video games), and other incredible technological advances. As a result, the United States has become a society more and more used to having practically anything—from food to news or information—quickly and conveniently. Much of this fast-paced provision of U.S. citizens' wants is based upon automated systems which "think" for their owners and eliminate the need for a human mind at certain points of production or operation. Many assert this has given citizens more free time, and there is undoubtedly some truth to the claim.

Yet, one might could also argue there is a danger to the increasingly automated nature of the American society. Children find electronic imaginary creations on video games as more fun than learning about their nation's history. Adults receive brief emailed articles from news media outlets and perceive whatever is in those articles as truth, without studying other opinions of the matter and judging for themselves. Media sources report and comment on candidates' speeches or promises, and many listeners and readers fail to check if the media or the candidates are correct in their assertions. There seems to be a growing acceptance by citizens of whatever is fed to them as truth or fact by computers or media or the popular opinion. This adds to a cycle of apathy by encouraging passivity in current affairs while also existing because of the already existing apathy of many Americans.

Independence cannot exist without individuals who think for themselves. "If a nation expects to be ignorant and free, in a state of civilization, it expects what never was and never will be," according to Thomas Jefferson.[20] There are endless possibilities with the great technological advances which seem to occur practically each day. IPhones can be utilized to read news articles practically anywhere. Instead of allowing the automated society to dictate one's perspectives and opinions, U.S. citizens should use these as opportunities to find information for themselves. Independence is not an attitude of refusing to accept the norm or rebelliously disagreeing with establishment or wisely and widely accepted standards. Independence is a self-sufficiency accomplished through a personal understanding of life from individual thinking and observation; this kind of independence results in a strong society of citizens who are interested in current affairs and who understand they are critical to the success of their government and, therefore, the future of the nation—a strong society of citizens who understand independence is a responsibility to respect.

# PART II:
## THE LAWS OF INDEPENDENCE

# 5

## THE U.S. CONSTITUTION CONSTRUED

Independent thinking did not see its end with the American victory in the War for Independence. The Articles of Confederation were written to provide a national government for the United States. Although the new U.S. citizens no longer suffered from tyranny, they soon realized they could create an even better system of government. In 1787, fifty-five men returned to the site of the signing of the Declaration of Independence, determined to create a new, permanent system of government.[21]

George Washington—the man credited for winning the American Revolution—was unanimously elected on May 25 as the president of the Constitutional Convention. Their actions over the next business day, according to James Madison's detailed notes, were focused upon setting the rules by which debate and deliberation would occur.[22] Clearly, these men understood the importance of respecting order and one another. In the end, these delegates to the Constitutional Convention unanimously voted for the U.S. Constitution. The convention's independent thinking and incredible attention to detail resulted in a document which—combined with the Bill of Rights—has proven its authors' forethought and wisdom through its effective, unique governing of a nation for over two hundred years with few alterations.

Yet, the exact meaning of certain phrases has tripped the nation considerably, as each of the three branches has attempted to remain subject to this Supreme Law of the Land while asserting its full authority over the people and its fellow branches. Hundreds of pages of commentary, hours upon hours of debate and discussion, and likely thousands of opinions have been written and voiced regarding these areas of controversy over the past two centuries. It is critical that the nation's citizens do not metaphorically throw their hands in the air in despair and cease to care how their Constitution is interpreted by the government. In reality, much of this debate and discussion can be narrowed into one main issue with two primary sides or opinions.[23]

The question is how to interpret the Constitution. One belief held by many—often called the "Living Constitution Theory" (or other names, including legal positivism, non-interpretivism, revisionism, etc.)—views the Constitution as a living document—one that changes and evolves over the course of history, along with the evolving, changing nature of society. To many, this sounds attractive and seems to make some practical sense. The origination of the more formal Living Constitution Theory was at Harvard University, about ten years after the beginning of Charles Darwin's propagation of his theory of evolution. Christopher Columbus Langdell was the first Harvard Law School dean; he believed in evolution and permitted his philosophy/religious thinking to permeate his lectures as he instructed students—thereby, creating additional lawyers who believed in evolutionary thinking as the appropriate perspective on law. (By the 1930s, the majority of legal scholars prescribed to this theory; it is highly likely this evolution in legal thought brought about the Constitutional Revolution of 1937 [see the next chapter].) In summary, those who follow this theory believe a document written over two hundred years ago could not be seen as absolutely authoritative when culture and society has changed so drastically.

Those who believe the opposite—often called strict constructionists (interprevists, etc.)—see danger in the Living Constitution Theory. They believe the authors of the Constitution meant what they said when they wrote the document. They believe in following the "letter of the law"—in the concept of the rule of law, asserting that a law is useless unless it is followed. Authoring a law is even more useless if it is not to be strictly enforced. In answer to living Constitution theorists' claims regarding society, the strict constructionists might agree with the fact that society has changed but would instead assert that the Constitution's authors wrote the document based on foundational truths regarding the governance of a society—as proven by hundreds of years of history. They would also point out that the Constitution does permit amendments to be ratified by the states.

It might seem these two theories hardly affect U.S. citizens' daily lives. In fact, many know little about the United States Constitution due to this belief of its insignificance to the average citizen. But nothing could be farther from the truth. The instructions or direction given in each article of the Constitution attempt to set the boundaries for the power of each of the three branches—in hopes of preventing tyranny and of protecting a system of government created by "We, the People." The content of anything written cannot be changed "so long as the material on which it was written [and copies of it] endures"; likewise, written documents have the ability to be passed down from generation to generation, thus ensuring that the words are preserved and respected.[24] The authors and signers of the Constitution believed their written words would be followed and would create the best system of government that man could envision.

The next two chapters analyze certain phrases or portions of this concrete document which have been considered controversial or have been ignored, altered, or otherwise less than accurately interpreted over the past several decades. One truth seems evident. If a recipe is written for a certain type of cake, and the cook desires to make that type of cake, the cook should follow the recipe closely. Any significant alteration or even an accumulation of small changes to the recipe will result in a different kind of cake than the one for which the recipe was written. If the United States of America wishes to remain the nation it has been for over two centuries—the federal republic wisely created by a group of men with great forethought—the three branches of government responsible for establishing, upholding, and interpreting the laws must follow the "recipe" provided by the Framers.

These chapters about law are included in a book regarding independence because without laws, there is no true independence. As John Locke once included in his writings, "'Where there is no law there is no freedom.'"[25] Without a knowledge of these laws and their meaning, there is no true independence. As already mentioned, Jefferson eloquently stated this truth by saying, "If a nation expects to be ignorant and free, in a state of civilization, it expects what never was and never will be."[26] If U.S. citizens wish to preserve the liberty they and their ancestors have enjoyed for over two centuries, they must first know and comprehend the laws which have ensured this great liberty and the dangers threatening them and then be ready to make use of these laws' provisions to defend the laws and the independence created by them.

# 6

## CLAUSES FOR CONCERN

One of the most key and controversial phrases in the U.S. Constitution is the "necessary and proper clause," found in Article I, Section 8. In explaining congressional power, the necessary and proper clause (or elastic clause) states that Congress shall have the power "to make all Laws which shall be necessary and proper for carrying into Execution the foregoing Powers, and all other Powers vested by this Constitution in the Government of the United States, or in any Department or Officer thereof." On face value and without taking into consideration other portions of the Constitution, this appears to be a complete and total surrender of power from the people and their states to Congress to make any and all laws it deems needed for completing its duties.

Anti-Federalists—those who opposed components of the Constitution before its ratification—expressed great alarm at such a clause. They feared it would result in the very evil they had liberated themselves from—tyranny.[27] Alexander Hamilton, a Federalist (one who favored the proposed Constitution), was one of the authors of the *Federalist Papers*—an excellent compilation of articles rebutting arguments made against the Constitution and explaining how (at least a number of) the signers of the Constitution interpreted their own document.

In *Federalist No. 33*, Hamilton explained his understanding of the necessary and proper clause with the following:

> They [the necessary and proper clause and a similar clause called the supremacy clause] are only declaratory of a truth which would have resulted by necessary and unavoidable implication from the very act of constituting a federal government, and vesting it with certain specified powers. ... What is a power, but the ability or faculty of doing a thing? What is the ability to do a thing, but the power of employing the MEANS necessary to its execution? What is a LEGISLATIVE power, but a power of making LAWS? What are the MEANS to execute a LEGISLA-TIVE power but LAWS? What is the power of laying and collecting taxes, but a LEGISLATIVE POWER, or a power of MAKING LAWS, to lay and collect taxes? What are the propermeans [sic] of executing such a power, but NECESSARY and PROPER laws?[28]

The above provided little comfort to those who feared the Congress would still utilize the clause as a "loophole" for legalizing tyranny. Hamilton expected or had already heard this concern and provided his take on those fears with the following from *Federalist No. 33*:

> But it may be again asked, Who is to judge of the NE-CESSITY and PROPRIETY of the laws to be passed for executing the powers of the Union? ... I answer, in the second place, that the national government, like every other, must judge, in the first instance, of the proper exercise of its powers, and its constituents in the last. If the federal government should overpass the just bounds of its authority and make a tyrannical use of its powers, the people, whose creature it is, must appeal to the standard

they have formed, and take such measures to redress the injury done to the Constitution as the exigency may suggest and prudence justify.[29]

In other words, Hamilton believed that the people still retained control of the government—their "creature"—through methods for which they provided in the Constitution (voting, etc.). Rather than viewing the government as the people's creature that, once given power, it could not be restrained—that it controlled the people—the Framers instead believed that the people were the government's ultimate source of authority...a power the people could evoke by revoking individual congressional members' power at any time (via the ballot). Clearly, the signers of the Constitution believed it would be interpreted as a whole—taking into consideration all portions of the document at the same time...rather than picking and choosing phrases or clauses as one does dishes in a buffet line. The following chapter highlights amendments to the Constitution which relate and explain the meaning the Framers expected the necessary and proper clause to have.

Another highly controversial clause is the "general welfare clause" found in Article I, Section 8, Clause 1—which is the following: "The Congress shall have Power To lay and collect Taxes, Duties, Imposts and Excises, to pay the Debts and provide for the common Defence [sic] and general Welfare of the United States; but all Duties, Imposts and Excises shall be uniform throughout the United States ...." While this might appear to be a full grant of power to Congress, again such claims are refuted by a Federalist and author of the *Federalist Papers*. *Federalist No. 41*, written by James Madison (a future President of the United States), explains the intended meaning of this clause. Madison claims the following:

It has been urged and echoed, that the power "to lay and

collect taxes, duties, imposts, and excises, to pay the debts, and provide for the common defense and general welfare of the United States," amounts to an unlimited commission to exercise every power which may be alleged to be necessary for the common defense or general welfare. ... Had no other enumeration or definition of the powers of the Congress been found in the Constitution, than the general expressions just cited, the authors of the objection might have had some color [substance or credibility] for it [the opposing argument]; though it would have been difficult to find a reason for so awkward a form of describing an authority to legislate in all possible cases. A power to destroy the freedom of the press, the trial by jury, or even to regulate the course of descents, or the forms of conveyances, must be very singularly expressed by the terms "to raise money for the general welfare." But what color can the objection have, when a specification of the objects alluded to by these general terms immediately follows, and is not even separated by a longer pause than a semicolon? If the different parts of the same instrument ought to be so expounded, as to give meaning to every part which will bear it, shall one part of the same sentence be excluded altogether from a share in the meaning; and shall the more doubtful and indefinite terms be retained in their full extent, and the clear and precise expressions be denied any signification whatsoever? For what purpose could the enumeration of particular powers be inserted, if these and all others were meant to be included in the preceding general power? Nothing is more natural nor common than first to use a general phrase, and then to explain and qualify it by a recital of particulars.[30]

Another revealing study would be the history of legislation and the Supreme Court's interpretation of various laws;

in summary, the Supreme Court did not view congressional power as essentially unlimited in its ability to regulate the American people and the states until what is often called the Constitutional Revolution of 1937 (see this chapter's later discussion of the commerce clause for a brief explanation of this historical event). Since the Constitutional Revolution of 1937, the Supreme Court has continually viewed congressional power as extremely broad, often establishing its findings in either or both of the two clauses mentioned above, as well as others.

Yet, specifically in response to the broad interpretations of the general welfare clause, one can argue welfare includes—such as according to the *Merriam-Webster Online Dictionary*—health, happiness, good fortune, and prosperity.[31] But one also can easily ask, especially given the quotations from the *Federalist Papers* above, if the Framers were truly saying that Congress had the power to ensure the health, happiness, and prosperity of each and every citizen in the United States—or merely the nation as a whole. The general welfare clause is in the same sentence as the reference to the common defense. It appears that the entire phrase is clearly referring to Congress's powers to accomplish purposes for the nation as a whole. Given a close study of the language and the Framer's intentions, it seems logical to assume the general welfare clause is not a wholesale grant of power to Congress to arrange for any purpose or program that would guarantee the health, happiness, and good fortune of each and every citizen. What about the drug addict whose happiness is only maintained by consuming illegal drugs, or the terrorist whose ultimate joy is murdering innocent?[32] That as the true meaning of the general welfare clause (the health, happiness, and prosperity of each and every citizen), to borrow Marshall's language in *Marbury v. Madison* (a case about another matter), "is too extravagant to be maintained."[33]

One could also argue that providing for the health of the nation as a whole requires or allows for programs such as a government-run healthcare system to be authorized, despite that such legislation so greatly infringes on the individuals' rights to make personal decisions free from government intervention. (Health care will be discussed more thoroughly in a further chapter.) If it is true that providing for the health of the nation as a whole necessitates a government-run healthcare system, why then cannot federal legislation be passed that says a citizen cannot marry prior or past a certain age—if that is deemed beneficial to the happiness of the nation? Why then cannot federal legislation be passed that dictates how many students per year can graduate with specific types of degrees—if such a measure were deemed beneficial to the well-being of the nation, in helping with equality or competition or economic goals? Again, as noted by the Framers, the Constitution was intended to be a document as a whole. As Madison so clearly stated, "shall one part of the same sentence be excluded altogether from a share in the meaning; and shall the more doubtful and indefinite terms be retained in their full extent, and the clear and precise expressions be denied any signification whatsoever?" Should one small, general phrase—the general welfare clause or any other, for that matter—be extracted from the more explicit remainder of the document?[34]

A similar controversy arises from the commerce clause found in Article 1, Section 8; this clause states that Congress has the authority "to regulate commerce with foreign nations, and among the several states, and with the Indian tribes." The center of the confusion and conflict is the phrase "among the several States." At the time of the writing and ratifying of the Constitution, states were establishing trade barriers and tariffs to impede the trade between states. In the landmark Supreme Court case *Gibbons v. Ogden*, Chief Justice John Marshall—

a man who would define the understanding of key elements of the Constitution—authored the Opinion of the Court and clearly settled that "among the several states" did not include internal commerce within each state (intrastate commerce).[35] Yet, in this case and others, Marshall and the other members of the Court also upheld the Constitution's intent on preventing such protectionist policies as placing special taxes on goods imported from other states (see *Brown v. Maryland*[36]). Over the next several years, there was a continual conflict among Congress, states, and the Supreme Court regarding the breadth of the federal government's power to regulate commerce. States persistently fought for their intrastate powers, and Congress insisted on broadening its power to regulate unfair business practices. One could say, in summary, that the Supreme Court attempted for decades to keep some semblance of states' rights to regulate their own internal commerce (intrastate), as appears to have been the literal meaning or original intent of the phrase.

Yet, as indicated above, the Constitutional Revolution of 1937 (caused in large part by evolutionary thought), the Great Depression, and a powerful, popular president and his threats resulted in the Supreme Court's interpretation of the commerce clause as essentially a grant of full power over all commerce, whether interstate or intrastate, to Congress. The landmark cases of this era were *Schechter Poultry Corp. v. United States* and *Carter v. Carter Coal Company*—in which the Court continued to uphold states' rights.[37] These cases so greatly angered President Franklin D. Roosevelt (particularly *Carter Coal*) that he formulated his unpopular court-packing plan. He threatened to change the composition of the Supreme Court, suggesting that every justice over the age of seventy be forced to retire, that a junior justice be added for every justice over seventy years old, and other similar ideas. The chief justice of the Supreme Court, Charles Evans Hughes, worked heavily behind the scenes, even composing a statistical document to prove the current justices' competency. The Court's composition was not changed, as Congress and the nation refused to follow FDR's suggestions; yet, the Supreme Court did not ignore FDR's wrath. In *National Labor Relations Board v. Jones & Laughlin Steel Corporation* (the landmark case of the Constitutional Revolution of 1937), the Court took the new road of broadening federal power over states.[38]

This new understanding of the commerce clause resulted in such decisions as *Wickard v. Filburn*.[39] In *Wickard v. Filburn*, Roscoe Filburn was a farmer who was accustomed to growing a little wheat, primarily for his personal consumption and the maintenance his farm; he usually sold his unused wheat. The Agricultural Adjustment Act of 1938 (a part of the New Deal) limited how much wheat farmers could grow to sell, based on their acreage and other factors. Filburn's limit was eleven acres; he sowed twenty-three acres, planning to sell only the eleven acres' wheat and keep the remainder for his own private, personal use. (The amount he kept for himself was valued to be slightly over $100.) Yet, the Department of Agriculture fined him. The Supreme Court agreed with the federal government, upholding the claim that Filburn should not have grown more wheat than the established eleven acres—even though the extra wheat was for his own private usage—because he would have otherwise had to purchase wheat from someone else, thereby affecting interstate commerce. In effect, the Court ruled that the federal government could tell farmers they could not grow wheat on their own private property for their own personal use, because such activity affected interstate commerce (commerce "among the several states")—an activity under the full authority of Congress. This ruling is clearly broad and alarming. Under this interpretation, Congress could theoretically pass legislation that controlled essentially any activity that affected one's purchase decisions—since every purchase affects the commerce of multiple states. It is quite difficult to imagine such an interpretation being envisioned by the Framers of the Constitution. Many Founding Fathers agreed with much of John Locke's theories and writings. John Locke once said that "… Government has no other end than the preservation of Property …."[40]

A similar, alarming trend of increasing federal power has continued during the past several decades. The first Supreme Court case in six decades to reject the federal government's claim of power under the commerce clause was *U.S. v. Lopez* in 1995. While, the Supreme Court has the authority to interpret the Supreme Law of the land, the people have the responsibility to elect members of Congress who respect that Supreme Law of the land and who will not attempt to pass legislation which usurps their constitutional authority. Under the Constitution, the American public too has the right to attempt to amend the Constitution, and thus overrule a Supreme Court decision or at least provide additional guidance to the Court. Yet, the best way to ensure the Court's sound judgment and an accurate reading of the U.S. Constitution is to elect presidents who will nominate and U.S. Senate members who will appoint sound Supreme Court justices. As U.S. Supreme Court Justice Hugo Black once said, "The public welfare demands that constitutional cases must be decided according to the terms of the Constitution itself, and not according to judges' views of fairness, reasonableness, or justice."[41] Protections against tyranny and limits on a naturally power-hungry government were imbedded in the words of the U.S. Constitution. How will the Constitution remain a protector of independence and liberty if the people which give it authority are ignorant of its provisions and of the attempts made to usurp it?

# 7

## MALLEABLE MEANINGS

If a doctor prescribes an antibiotic that must be taken three times a day, a person who wishes to get well will follow what the prescription actually says. The fact that the prescription does not say the antibiotic cannot be taken six times a day or even all at once does not give the patient the "liberty" to do so. On a similar note, the Constitution does contain a clear enumeration of Congress's powers. It also includes phrases such as the ones previously discussed, which are not as specific. Returning to the prescription analogy, what if the prescription specifies that the antibiotic be taken with food? That gives a patient great liberty. The patient can take the antibiotic with ice cream, beef, chicken, or whatever food she wishes; she can take the medicine with a meal or with a snack. Yet, a basic reading of the words does not imply that merely because the prescription says a patient can take the medicine with "food," the patient should eat all the food she can find each time she takes the medicine. (That, of course, would make the patient sick.) Likewise, as already discussed, merely because the Constitution says Congress can provide for the general welfare of the United States does not mean that it should do everything that it can possibly do to improve the wellbeing of the nation; that would make for a very sick nation. Similarly, as also addressed above, Congress's power to make all laws necessary and proper for carrying out its specified powers is not the power to make all laws; it qualifies that statement with the phrase "necessary and proper" for its specific powers, as analyzed earlier.

Yet, these are not the only truths and practical perspectives regarding the Constitution that argue for a more literal interpretation of the document. Just as a prescription will sometimes even specify that the antibiotic should be taken with a meal rather than just food or eight ounces of water (therefore, excluding a small snack or ten ounces of milk), the Bill of Rights contains both the Ninth and Tenth Amendments which specify additional limits on federal power. The Ninth Amendment states, "The enumeration in the Constitution, of certain rights, shall not be construed to deny or disparage others retained by the people." This clearly calls for a limited reading of the powers of the federal government enumerated in the Constitution. It clearly implies that the enumeration of powers was meant to be understood as a specific listing of powers, rather than merely a few examples; it acknowledges there are understood rights reserved to the people, upon which the government has no (expressed, implied, or inherent) power to infringe. (One can hardly imagine a Framer appreciating the idea of the federal government's telling him how to handle his healthcare.)

Even if the Ninth Amendment was not enough to make the government's limited power clear, the Tenth Amendment additionally sets the government's boundaries. The Tenth Amendment states, "The powers not delegated to the United States by the Constitution, nor prohibited by it to the States, are reserved to the States respectively, or to the people." Here, the Framers flatly establish that the powers which the Constitution did not specifically give to the federal government (or prohibit the states from exercising) are powers which belong to the people and the states. Another reading of the phrase is simply that the powers given to the federal government in the Constitution are the powers of the federal government—no more and no less.

Yet, as noted above, the Supreme Court has upheld the significant broadening of Congress's power, particularly in the arena of commerce. Modern society—and, in reality, society since the 1930s—has suggested that the American people ignore the restrictions on the government included in the Constitution and the Bill of Rights. U.S. citizens must not continue this blissful ignorance, or more and more of their rights will be continue to be gradually surrendered to an ever power-hungry government, as it portrays itself as merely a provider of the wants of its citizens. Thomas Jefferson best described what clearly was intended to be the interpretation of the Constitution and the Tenth Amendment in the following quotations:

I consider the foundation of the Constitution as laid on this ground: That "all powers not delegated to the United States, by the Constitution, nor prohibited by it to the States, are reserved to the States or to the people" [10th Amendment]. To take a single step beyond the boundaries thus specifically drawn around the powers of Congress is to take possession of a boundless field of power, no longer susceptible of any definition.

It [is] inconsistent with the principles of civil liberty, and contrary to the natural rights of the other members of the society, that any body of men therein should have authority to enlarge their own powers... without restraint.

Though written constitutions may be violated in moments of passion or delusion, yet they furnish a text to which those who are watchful may again rally and recall the people. They fix, too, for the people the principles of their political creed.

Unless the mass retains sufficient control over those entrusted with the powers of their government, these will be perverted to their own oppression, and to the perpetuation of wealth and power in the individuals and their families selected for the trust. [. . .][42]

It is clearly the responsibility of the American people to hold the government accountable for its proper and improper usage of the power given to it by the people. When asked about how he felt regarding the recently passed health care reform's constitutionality, a Democratic congressman answered, "I don't worry about the Constitution on this" (he proceeded to confuse the Constitution and the Declaration of Independence; when his mistake was noted, he replied, "Doesn't matter to me. Either one").[43] Such an attitude from an elected official—who would have no power to make laws without the Supreme Law of the Land—should arouse the concern of every U.S. citizen. Such an attitude leaves plenty of room for every abuse of power and every infringement of individual liberties attempted to be prevented by the Framers as they signed the Constitution.

The following quotation by John Locke provides a very relevant description of the purpose of government:

The Care therefore of every man's Soul belongs unto himself, and is to be left unto himself. But what if he neglect the Care of his Soul? I answer, What if he neglect the Care of his Health, or of his Estate, which things are nearlier [sic] related to the Government of the Magistrate than the other? Will the Magistrate provide by an express

Law, that such an one shall not become poor or sick? Laws provide, as much as is possible, that the Goods and Health of Subjects be not injured by the Fraud and Violence of others; they do not guard them from the Negligence or Ill-husbandry of the Possessors themselves.[44]

As the following two chapters will demonstrate, and as the above chapters have indicated, the government by nature has over the past several decades successfully gained more and more control over individuals' lives and has time and time again arguably overstepped its constitutional bounds. Regardless of the noble end intended, good accomplished, or the evil prevented by a number of these laws, the trend is still obvious and should still be noted. "Freedom is the sure possession of those who have the courage to defend it."[45] Independence—U.S. citizens who cherish it must use it and protect it.

# 8

## THE BAILOUT BILL: "BAILING OUT" ON THE AMERICAN PEOPLE

As discussed earlier, independence depends upon a society's remaining informed about its government, legislation, and current events. Below is a study completed by this author in 2009 (a portion of which was published in pamphlet form), not long after the passage of the "America Recovery and Reinvestment Act of 2009," often called the "Recovery Act" or the "bailout bill."[46] President Barack Obama and the media attempted to portray the legislation as an economic victory, set to save the nation from sure disaster. Yet, the facts contradict such an assertion, as explained below.

"Our country faces its most serious economic crisis since the Great Depression," according to President Barack Obama's website, obama-recovery-plan.com.[47] This negative outlook was the prevailing attitude of the American public, media, and presidency in the early months of 2009. The reader is urged to take a step back to the Great Depression—the supposed near twin of the state of U.S. economy in early 2009. Franklin D. Roosevelt became president with promises to end the Great Depression; he created the "New Deal," which involved the creation of a larger government bureaucracy with a promise of more jobs and more prosperity. Many hail FDR as the man who saved the nation from the Great Depression. Will Obama forever be hailed as the man who saved the nation from its "Second Great Depression?" Some people seem to believe so, and many wish to compare the two men. The following is one author's opinion:

> There are some very powerful analogies and similarities between the two men [FDR and Obama]. They both ran against an unpopular Republican Party and, as times got hard, promised to be much more interventionist than activist. They were both incredibly charismatic figures; they ran on a promise of hope and taking bold action; they're both great communicators; and also they have similar skills of reaching out to a broad coalition. ... And I think as Obama takes office, there's also a sense that he intends to be very pragmatic, almost to follow FDR's edict of experimentation—try something and if it doesn't work, try something else. So I think it's a very apt analogy between the two men and a good one because we sort of need an FDR figure right now.[48]

Yet, living conditions in May 2009 for the average U.S. citizen are not nearly as terrible as the conditions survived by those living during the depths of the Great Depression.

Nevertheless, as mentioned above, Obama's website urges the parallelism between today and the 1930s. Only a few months into his presidency, Obama claims to have, with his vice president Joe Biden,

> already put together a plan to revitalize the economy:
> 1. Immediate action to create good jobs in america [sic].
> 2 Immediate relief for struggling families.
> 3. Direct, immediate assistance for homeowners and busi-

ness owners.

4. Rapid, aggressive response to our financial crisis, using tools such as Government Grants.[49]

A major tool of this plan was the passage of the American Recovery and Reinvestment Act of 2009. One source's count found this piece of legislation to be 1,588 pages in length.[50] One congressional member claims "members of Congress had less than 12 hours to review over 1,200 pages of federal government largesse before voting on it today [February 13, 2009]. ... The entire process for crafting this massive bill – the largest spending bill in the history of the US – was done in secret, behind closed doors...."[51] The Small Business Administration provides the following summary of this omnibus bill:

> The American Recovery and Reinvestment Act of 2009 (Recovery Act) was signed into law by President Obama on February 17, 2009. It is an unprecedented effort to jumpstart our economy, create or save millions of jobs, and put a down payment on addressing long-neglected challenges so our country can thrive in the 21st century. The Act is an extraordinary response to a crisis unlike any since the Great Depression, and includes measures to modernize our nation's infrastructure, enhance energy independence, expand educational opportunities, preserve and improve affordable health care, provide tax relief, and protect those in greatest need.[52]

Although many praise the New Deal policies of FDR and encourage President Barack Obama to follow in the footsteps of this Great Depression president, the American Recovery and Reinvestment Act of 2009 and the reasoning behind it do not promote the general welfare of the American people and, in

51

reality, "bail out" on American citizens and their children and their future because of its neglect of ethical fiscal principles supported by history's leaders, its indirect but real threat to the United States' security, and its faulty economic reasoning and the reality of economic fundamentals.

Interest on borrowed money is an interesting phenomenon. "Interest works day and night, in fair weather and in foul. It gnaws at a man's substance with invisible teeth," according to Henry Ward Beecher.[53] In addition, "it is money that in a sense is paying for nothing."[54] Albert Einstein once said, "The most powerful force in the universe is compound interest."[55] If one truly considers this concept, it is not difficult to believe. Once families become too entangled in high interest rates (particularly those charged by credit card companies), life is a constant struggle to keep from drowning in debt. Imagine if a couple with two adult children found themselves in such a position of an ever growing debt load, but the parents continued to spend more and more borrowed funds. After their death, their children were left with the heavy burden of their parents' spending and interest. Imagine another couple with two young children who had reckless borrowing and spending habits and who eventually lost everything they owned—including many of their children's belongings. The parents' debt basically became their children's, as their children also had to give up toys, friends, and other "treasures." The children did not have to pay their parents' debt with cash; but they still had to part with items, memories, and possibly even people of value to them.

What if there was a country in the world in which young children were having to work to provide funding for their parents' endless spending and borrowing, or college graduates' earnings were being used to pay for purchases and loans that were not their own but were their parents'? In "Main Street America," most adults, if they find themselves in serious debt, have to pay off that debt at some point; the laws prohibit them from spending and borrowing for years and years without ever suffering any consequences of defaulting on a loan. They are required at some point to face their debts, either by repaying the borrowed funds and accumulated interest or by watching the seizure of their belongings. Most parents are not permitted to "bail out" on their children; it is expected that parents pay off their own debts as much as possible. It is the moral and ethical action to take.

Every citizen—every man, woman, and child—in the United States of America on May 21, 2009, owed approximately $37,000 to creditors from whom they have never borrowed—whom they have never met and never contacted.[56] This exorbitant debt is not due to any purchases of their own; this does not include any debt they have incurred themselves when purchasing a home, car, or other necessary item. The national debt on May 21, 2009, was approximately $11 trillion—growing at a rate of approximately $100,000 every second or two.[57] In the early 1990s, President Bill Clinton attempted to improve the struggling health care system but was unsuccessful, partly due to "a widespread perception that the plan might make the deficit even worse"; the total national deficit over which concern was being expressed was only $290 billion.[58] In other words, only recently, the words *millions* and *billions* of dollars raised eyebrows; if Congress passed a piece of legislation providing *billions* of dollars to a particular project or war or situation, it was notable. In the early months of 2009, billions of dollars became practically "small change"; *trillion* became the common word of Congressional appropriations, despite the already massive debt the United States had accumulated.

"CBO [Congressional Budget Office] and JCT [Joint Committee on Taxation] estimate that enacting H.R. 1 [American Recovery and Reinvestment Act of 2009] would increase budget deficits by $526 billion over the 2009-2010 period (about 19 months) and by a total of $816 billion over the 2009-2019 period"; this was the estimate for the January 26, 2009 version of the Recovery Act.[59] By February 13, 2009, one source reported the Recovery Act to have total expenditures of $850 billion.[60] Yet, what is reality? According to Congressman Paul Ryan and the information provided to him by the CBO two weeks prior to the Recovery Act's passage, interest on the borrowed funds for H.R. 1 (the $820 billion version) would increase the nation's debt load by another $347 billion, resulting in a total cost of over $1.2 trillion for the Recovery Act. In addition, provisions of the omnibus spending bill call for "abrupt, and sharp, spending reductions after two years" for certain programs; "these programs include health care benefits for the unemployed, early childhood education, nutrition programs for seniors, and funding for state and local law enforcement agencies." Ryan speculates that "due to immense pressure that will mount to maintain the funding levels in these programs, the reductions are highly unlikely to occur. As Milton Friedman presciently lamented, 'Nothing is so permanent as a temporary government program.'" Assuming Ryan's speculations prove to be correct in two years, the Recovery Act's $820 billion plus another $1.7 trillion will be necessary; with interest of $745 billion on the $1.7 trillion, the result will be a total cost of $3.27 trillion for the Recovery Act (a debt load of approximately $30,000 for each U.S. family).[61] This is true, while almost $37,000 per U.S. citizen had already accumulated by late May of 2009 (as noted above). In other words, Congress and Obama have chosen to not only ignore the already massive debt, due to be grappled with by future generations, but also add to it. The following statement made by one of the nation's founding fathers—Benjamin Franklin—seems fitting in this context: "Tis against some men's principle to pay interest, and seems against others' interest to pay the principle [sic]."[62]

It is common sense that one trying to help a person with his or her spending problem or habit does not give the struggling individual hundreds of dollars more. People with spending problems and true friends are likely to hear statements similar to the following wise sayings by Franklin: "Rather go to bed supperless than rise in debt"; "let honesty and industry be thy constant companions, and spend one penny less than thy clear gains; then shall thy pocket begin to thrive; creditors will not insult, nor want oppress, nor hungerness bite, nor nakedness freeze thee."[63] "Virtually everyone agrees that we need to further stimulate the economy even though current attempts to solve our crisis by increasing spending is exactly the wrong thing to do. ... You can't solve an excessive spending problem by spending more. We are making the crisis worse," assert Lawrence H. White and David C. Rose, two economic professors.[64] Franklin also warned, "beware of little expenses; a small leak will sink a great ship."[65] When even a small leak can sink a great ship, should there not be great concern about a large leak?

Franklin is not the only historical leader to which one can turn regarding this matter of spending too much. Alexander Hamilton—the nation's first Treasury Secretary and a co-author of the *Federalist Papers*—supported the concept of a public debt, yet he conditioned his support with these assertions:

> That exigencies are to be expected to occur in the affairs of nations, in which there will be a necessity for borrowing. That loans in times of public danger, especially from foreign war, are found an indispensable resource, even to the wealthiest of them [nations]. ... And as on the one hand, the necessity for borrowing, in particular emergencies, cannot be doubted, so on the other it is equally evident

that to be able to borrow, upon good terms, it is essential that the credit of a nation should be well established. .... If maintenance of public credit, then, be truly so important, the next inquiry which suggests itself is, by what means is it to be effected? The ready answer to which question is, by good faith, by a punctual performance of contracts. States, like individuals, who observe their engagements, are respected and trusted; while the reverse is the fate of those who pursue an opposite conduct. Every breach of the public engagements, whether from choice or necessity, is in different degress [sic: degrees] hurtful to public credit. When such a necessity does truly exist, the evils of it are only to be palliated by a scrupulous attention, on the part of the Government, to carry the violation no further than the necessity absolutely requires, and to manifest, if the nature of the case admits of it, a sincere disposition to make reparation whenever circumstances shall permit.[66]

In summary of Hamilton's remarks, just as an individual is esteemed for repaying loans fully and promptly, so is a nation. Hamilton also acknowledges that, while detrimental, situations may compel a nation to not fully honor its loans' conditions. Even in such situations, this dishonorable behavior should be strictly limited to only that which is essential for survival; in addition, measures must be attempted to make amends for any such dishonorable behavior. As correctly stated in a book regarding American public policy, "limiting the occurrences of federal deficits and the amount of the national debt are serious goals for the United States because they show fiscal responsibility. In other words, they demonstrate the ability to live within one's means, an important political goal."[67] In summary, borrowing in an appropriate manner is a matter of ethical principles.

A likely response to this argument would be that Obama's

spending more than could truly ever be repaid has been his response to a critical national emergency. Whether or not there has truly been an emergency or whether or not the situation has been as serious as claimed is better addressed (to a limited degree) in a further section of this paper. Regardless, it is true the U.S. economy has been facing difficult times. While remembering the ethics of borrowing no more than necessary and borrowing no more than a nation could repay whenever possible, one might consider the details of the Recovery Act and determine if each provision was necessary to combating the economic "disaster" facing the nation. The reader should be made aware of the Recovery Act's tax credit for anyone who buys "a 'neighborhood electric vehicle'"—which, by law, can only travel up to speeds of 20 to 25 miles per hour—and may ponder its necessity in the battle against complete economic catastrophe; similarly, nothing forbids the Recovery Act's $144 billion to be used by state and local government officials from being spent on "any 'stadium, community park, museum, theater, art center, and highway beautification project.'"[68] Funding for "'the utilization of an electronic health record (EHR) for each person in the United States by 2014'" was also included in a February 11, 2009 version of the Recovery Act (which "also indicates that a doctor who is not a 'meaningful EHR user' in terms of using patients' health records to provide the most cost-efficient coverage could face penalties").[69] In late January 2009, it was reported that the Recovery Act provided funds ($5.2 billion) to ACORN, "the left-leaning nonprofit group under federal investigation for massive voter fraud."[70] One could easily ask why the federal government would provide funds to a group suspected of crime—especially such a politically charged crime.

Given the numbers above, it is natural to wonder how future generations of the U.S. could be expected to pay off such debt, which is continually growing. "The Obama administration has not produced a plan for returning to a sustainable spending path, which has troubled some economists, such as former federal budget director Alice Rivlin," according to Arnold Kling of the Cato Institute.[71] Congressman Jason Chaffetz asserts that "the federal government's long-term un-funded liabilities total nearly $57 trillion. This massive trillion dollar bill [the Recovery Act] adds to the crushing debt that each and every ... American will one day have to repay."[72]

The discussion begins to take another direction as one contemplates repayment of all these loans and borrowed funds with their interest; concerns of national security come to mind. One can turn once again to history—specifically post-World War I Germany—for comparison. "A truly runaway hyper-inflation" is caused in part by "... a large budget deficit that no one believes will be closed in the future," according to J. Bradford DeLong of the University of California at Berkeley; he further explains in the following:

> Faced with the prospect of budget deficits for as far ahead as the eye can see, the usual sources of credit to the government dry up; it can no longer borrow to cover the gap between revenues and expenditures. The only alternative is to print more and more banknotes. ... As the government continues to print money, inflation continues. And as the consciousness that your cash will be worth less tomorrow than it is today penetrates the minds of the public, the situation further deteriorates. If cash loses value the longer you hold it, you should spend it as fast as possible. ... Because to fail to spend cash is to waste its purchasing power..., price rises outstrip the rate of money creation....[73]

DeLong proceeds to say that after World War I, "the reparations question was made even more complicated because no one was sure what Germany would pay to the allies for losing the war, what it could pay, or what sanctions the allied powers would be willing to employ"; due to the economic trouble during the war and the reparations demanded after the war, "by the end of 1923 the German price level was 1,260,000,000,000 times what it had been at the start of World War I."[74] The official reparations total demanded of Germany as determined on April 27, 1921, was 132 billion gold marks.[75] This huge burden on the German people played a significant role in Hitler's rise to power and, subsequently, World War II. Fifty-seven to seventy-four German marks were equal to approximately one U.S. dollar in January of 1921.[76] Utilizing the fifty-seven marks value, simple arithmetic shows that Germany's required reparations were roughly the equivalent to $2.3 billion 1921 U.S. dollars. In 1921, a consumer price index calculator shows that one U.S. dollar would have had "the same buying power as $11.91 in 2009" (as of May 25, 2009).[77] Therefore, Germany's official reparations total was—in today's U.S. dollars—approximately $27.4 billion.[78] Compare that figure to the United States' current debt.

While the United States' creditors are clearly not demanding full repayment of borrowed funds (as of May 2009), what if they did? Would the U.S. find itself in a situation similar to post-WWI Germany's? A concerned citizen might attempt to comfort him/herself with the assumption that the United States' creditors would surely not be nations hostile to the USA—yet such an assumption is not actually fact. In March 2007, John W. Schoen of MSNBC.com discussed the debt then President George W. Bush was accumulating while fighting the war against terrorism. Schoen explains that in June 2006, the U.S. government was "the biggest holder of Treasury debt" (an explanation of this concept is beyond the scope of this paper). At that time, one fourth of the nation's debt (then $8.5 trillion) was "held by foreign governments." Schoen also responds to a concern expressed by then Senator and presidential candidate Hillary Clinton regarding "America's dependence on Chinese investors"; Schoen assures and warns his readers with the following:

> Foreign investment in the U.S.—in U.S. stocks, bonds, real estate and businesses—isn't necessarily a bad thing. ... What matters most is the ongoing strength of the U.S. economy and the federal government's financial health. To the extent that Congress can control spending, eliminate the federal budget deficit and keep the economy growing, we should be fine. ... But growth seems to be slowing and, at some point, the economy could slide into a recession. When that happens, the economy shrinks and so do tax revenues. But Uncle Sam still has to pay interest on what he's borrowed—just like you don't get a break on your mortgage payment when you lose your job. If we keep spending more and more on interest, the federal budget gets squeezed that much harder when the economy eventually stumbles. ... And as the cost of paying Social Security and Medicare benefits continues to rise, the national debt monster is going to be even harder to tame.[79]

As the reader knows, the United States has since suffered a recession; and government spending has not only continued but also increased. By November of 2008, an article appeared in the *Washington Post*, announcing the following:

> China passed Japan to become the U.S. government's largest foreign creditor in September.... China's new status – it now owns nearly $1 out of every $10 in U.S. public debt – means Washington will be increasingly forced to rely on Beijing as it seeks to raise money to cover the cost of a $700 billion bail out. China, in fact, may be the government's largest creditor, period. The treasury does not keep

records on domestic bond holders [sic]. But analysts said China's holdings are so vast that the existence of a larger stakeholder in the United States now seems unlikely.

The article proceeds to explain the various possibilities of China's selling or "moving out of" U.S. government bonds—which would result in true economic catastrophe (especially since "China is thought to be purchasing U.S. debt through third countries, purchases that are not immediately recorded by the Treasury as being held by China, analysts say").[80] On February 23, 2009, almost two years following Clinton's expression of concern regarding debt held by China and only ten days following the passage of the largest spending bill in U.S. history, an article appeared in Great Britain, stating, "US Secretary of State Hillary Clinton has pleaded with China to continue buying US Treasury bonds amid mounting fears that Washington may struggle to finance bank bail-outs and ballooning deficits over the next two years"; the article also reported that

the Treasury says it needs to raise almost $500bn [billion] (£350bn) in debt in the first quarter alone. Estimates for 2009 reach as high as $2 trillion, a huge sum in a world starved of capital at a time almost all the major governments are launching fiscal rescue packages.[81]

Clinton assured, "It's a safe investment. The United States has a well-deserved financial reputation."[82] One could easily wonder if the United States' financial reputation is in jeopardy.[83]

What if China chose to make decisions not in the best interest of the United States? Two different scenarios in which China's decisions could wreck havoc on the U.S. economy have already been noted. How likely are such detrimental decisions by the Chinese? There is no doubt China is a distant friend of the U.S.—at best; most times, China appears to be an enemy of freedom and, therefore, of the United States. In May 2009, according to the Associated Press, "China sharply restricts religious practices and controls activities of churches and mosques, the report from the congressionally backed U.S. Commission on International Religious Freedom said."[84] In addition, there has been criticism of "China's treatment of Tibetans and dissidents."[85] Most shocking was an April 2009 article in the *Wall Street Journal*, which reported the following:

> Cyperspies have penetrated the U.S. electrical grid and left behind software programs that could be used to disrupt the system, according to current and former national-security officials. The spies came from China, Russia and other countries, these officials said, and were believed to be on a mission to navigate the U.S. electrical system and its controls. The intruders haven't sought to damage the power grid or other key infrastructure, but officials warned they could try during a crisis or war. ... Officials said water, sewage and other infrastructure systems also were at risk. [86]

Why would a true friend of the United States wish to position itself so that it could easily sabotage the U.S.? The cyber-attacks are clearly a matter of national security. (According to the *Wall Street Journal*, "... a cyberattack had taken out power equipment in multiple regions outside the U.S."[87]) It would be natural for one to insist on the United States' countering such attacks. Yet, Clinton made the following valid point in 2007, which is all the more true today: "How do you get tough on your banker?"[88] One cannot argue with the following similar point found in the Bible: "The rich rules over the poor, And the borrower is servant to the lender."[89]

One might argue, "Focus on the economics; focus on the good Obama's Recovery Act will accomplish for so many millions of people, such as the economic good affected by Roosevelt's policies." The American public, as indicated earlier, has been told time and time again that the United States is suffering the worst economic downturn since the Great Depression—which was an economic disaster indeed. The media's comparisons between FDR and Obama have been numerous.

"Why doesn't Santy [sic] Claus come to see little boys whose daddies haven't jobs?" asked Freddie, a boy of five years of age—in 1934; in the *Richmond Times Dispatch*, on December 16, 1934, it was reported that common state of affairs for many children as Christmas approached and the Great Depression pressed upon the lives of so many, while urging people to give to the needy—as had many members of the "Good Fellows" club. The article's author pleads with her readers, as she illustrates the Great Depression life of a family of thirteen—"in danger of being evicted" and in possession of two blankets and two beds and with no income since September (and that was provided by one of the children). The article revealed, "The situation this year is acute. Six thousand remain on the club lists."[90]

FDR's New Deal has historically been hailed as the key to the end of the abundance of such pitiful stories as above. His New Deal had a "... tendency toward 'Keynesian' economic policies of revitalizing a mass-consumption based economy by revitalizing the masses [sic] ability to consume"; yet, "Roosevelt was a faint-hearted Keynesian, at best."[91] Regardless, what is Keynesian economics? N. Gregory Mankiw, a Harvard professor who advised Bush, explains John Maynard Keynes' theories in the following:

According to Keynes, the root cause of economic

downturns is insufficient aggregate demand. When the total demand for goods and services declines, businesses throughout the economy see their sales fall off. Lower sales induce firms to cut back production and to lay off workers. Rising unemployment and declining profits further depress demand, leading to a feedback loop with a very unhappy ending. The situation reverses, Keynesian theory says, only when some event or policy increases aggregate demand.[92]

Another source explains that Keynes believed this:

A slump was simply a short-run problem stemming from a lack of demand. If the private sector was not prepared to spend to boost demand, the government should instead. It could do this by running a budget deficit. When times were good again and the private sector was spending again, the government could trim its spending and pay off the debts they accumulated in the slump.[93]

In August 2004, two economists at the University of California at Los Angeles—Harold L. Cole and Lee E. Ohanian—announced that "… they have figured out why the Great Depression dragged on for almost 15 years, and they blame a suspect previously though to be beyond reproach: President Franklin D. Roosevelt." The following expands upon this observation and further discusses the professors' research:

Roosevelt's role in lifting the nation out of the Great Depression has been so revered that Time [sic] magazine readers cited it in 1999 when naming him the 20th century's second-most influential figure. "This is exciting and valuable research," said Robert E. Lucas Jr., [sic] the 1995 Nobel Laureate in economics, and the John

Dewey Distinguished Service Professor of Economics at the University of Chicago. "The prevention and cure of depressions is a central mission of macroeconomics, and if we can't understand what happened in the 1930s, how can we be sure it won't happen again?"

Ohanian asserts, "We found that a relapse isn't likely unless lawmakers gum up a recovery with ill-conceived stimulus policies"; "'President Roosevelt believed that excessive competition was responsible for the Depression by reducing prices and wages, and by extension reducing employment and demand for goods and services,' said Cole ...."[94] Close study of that summary reveals Roosevelt's underlying belief in Keynesian economics (that depressions result from insufficient demand). In summary of the New Deal, "'Roosevelt had some successes, but we hope that Obama is going to do better,' said Kenneth S. Rogoff, a professor of economics at Harvard. 'Otherwise, we're in trouble.'"[95]

While it appears there were no significant anti-competition provisions in Obama's Recovery Act (although it would be difficult to know for certain, given its large size), Obama's stimulus—the Recovery Act—undoubtedly seems to mesh with Keynes's belief in increased government spending at the time of an economic downturn (in the absence of sufficient public demand). Certainly, FDR's stimulus—the New Deal—also meshed with this Keynesian theory. From 1933 to 1940, government spending increased by 106 percent.[96] The approximate total cost of the New Deal between 1933 and 1940 was $50 billion.[97] One 1935 U.S. dollar would buy what $15.56 would buy today (utilizing a consumer price index calculator); in other words, today's dollar would only purchase an item worth only six cents in 1935.[98] Using the 1935 dollar, $50 billion would roughly purchase what $778 billion would today.

"There is no disagreement that we need action by our government, a recovery plan that will help to jumpstart the economy," claimed President-elect Barack Obama on January 9, 2009.[99] "With all due respect Mr. President, that is not true"—this response comes from a long list of economists, including Nobel laureates and professors from universities such as Harvard, Emory, Vanderbilt, Cornell, George Washington, George Mason, Auburn, Johns Hopkins, and Duke.[100] These economists assert, "Notwithstanding reports that all economists are now Keynesians and that we all support a big increase in the burden of government, we do not believe that more government spending is a way to improve economic performance." Their reasons include that "more government spending by Hoover and Roosevelt did not pull the United States economy out of the Great Depression in the 1930s."[101] One author asserts that "Keynesianism doesn't boost national income, it merely redistributes it"; "any money that the government puts in the economy's right pocket is money that is first removed from the economy's left pocket."[102] According to another author, cited by the *Washington Post*, "Roosevelt the economist is unworthy of emulation."[103] Ike Brannon (a former U.S. Treasury Senior Advisor) and Chris Edwards assert, "As Harvard University's Robert Barro noted in disapproval of the stimulus plan, just because the economy is in crisis, it does 'not invalidate everything we have learned about macroeconomics since 1936.'"[104]

In an article published in November 2008, N. Gregory Mankiw (a Harvard professor and advisor to President George W. Bush and presidential candidate Mitt Romney) expresses his concern that "increased government spending may be a good short-run fix, but it would add to the budget deficit. ... Any increase in the national debt will make fulfilling those unfunded promises [Medicare and Social Security claims] harder in the coming years." He continues with this observation:

Passing a larger national debt to the next generation may look attractive to those without children. (Keynes himself was childless.) But the rest of us cannot feel much comfort knowing that, in the long run, when we are dead, our children and grandchildren will be dealing with our fiscal legacy.[105]

The reader is urged to refer back to the Great Depression stories of children at Christmastime. While there are many American children who face sad holidays every year, whether or not the nation is in a recession, the United States is—as of May 2009—clearly not in the same situation as it was in the 1930s; the United States is not experiencing an economic slump of the Great Depression's magnitude. The reader is then urged to refer back to the spending figures of the two presidents. FDR's New Deal is estimated to have cost in a period of seven years approximately $778 billion in today's dollars; Obama's Recovery Act is estimated to cost over the next several years between $1.2 trillion and $3.27 trillion. Obama's spending is likely to continue, as indicated earlier, especially given remarks made by his Treasury Secretary Timothy Geithner in March 2009 ("Mr. Geithner didn't dismiss the possibility [of requesting more funds for banks] either").[106] On January 29, 2009, *The Wall Street Journal* reported that "government officials seeking to revamp the U.S. financial bailout have discussed spending another $1 trillion to $2 trillion to help restore banks to health, according to people familiar with the matter."[107] Similarly, Press Secretary Robert Gibbs said on February 18, 2009, regarding the possibility of another stimulus bill, "I wouldn't foreclose it."[108] In addition, as reported in *Newsweek* magazine on May 25, 2009, Obama's spending is not to decrease at all. The spending for Obama's proposed budget for 2010 was cleverly and vividly illustrated with an itemization of examples of what all could be purchased with the same amount of money Obama has proposed to spend; the following is the text of the illustration:

What can you buy with Obama's 2010 federal budget? **$2,399,000,000,000** (Everything produced in Italy in 2008) + **$781,000,000,000** (All the oil in Saudi Arabia) + **$146,118,655,260** (An electric car for every 16- and 17-year-old in America) + **$130,217,134,075** (The International Space Station) + **$65,000,000,000** (A refund for everyone defrauded by Bernie Madoff) + **$22,000,000,000** (The Big Dig, Boston's urban-infrastructure money pit) + **$4,000,000,000** (Full funding for the Krasnow Instittue's project to map the human brain) + **$1,839,150,000** (All the tea in China) + **$507,142,826** (The treasures of King Tut's tomb) + **$300,786,314** (One $.99 MP$_3$ download from iTunes for everyone in America) + **$13,592,218** (The first-ever weeklong staging of Stockhausen's seven-opera series) + **$2,350,000** (... a mint condition 1909 Honus Wagner [baseball card]) + **$1,189,000** (Recession-era bargain: an Upper East Side condo on 94th Street) + **$298.50** (Marc Jacobs 214S sunglasses [with dark gray lenses]) + **$8.50** (Carnitas burrito at Chipotle in Manhattan [plus tax]) = **$3,550,000,000,000**, Or we could just keep the country afloat. [Emphasis added for clarity.][109]

When the United States is not currently suffering as much as it was during the Great Depression, why should Obama spend even more than FDR did in futility in the 1930s, especially considering that economics proves FDR's large spending sprees did not actually end the Great Depression?

"The stimulus package [the Recovery Act] was a huge victory for Obama less than one month into his presidency. [. . .] 'None of this will be easy,' he [Obama] said. 'The road to recovery will not be straight. We will make progress, and there may be some slippage along the way.'"[110] It is without a doubt true that the United States economy has experienced a rough economic downturn. Yet, difficult times do not call for a neglect of ethics or principles, a blind eye to national security, or a refusal to acknowledge economic truths. Each of these was accomplished by the American Recovery and Reinvestment Act of 2009; its increase of our debt, its ignorance of danger, and its decision to guide the nation according to disproved economic theories is "bailing out" on the future generations of the United States. Hamilton and Franklin helped to found this nation, while holding valid views regarding sound fiscal policy—which they felt applied to both nations and individuals, and which many parents still teach their children today. Ignoring the national debt and instead dramatically and unhesitatingly increasing it to an amount that could never be repaid is not financially wise or economically sound—and could potentially be disastrous to the security of the nation, especially when the U.S. begs even enemy nations to serve as its creditors.

Many felt there was a need for change on Election Day 2008; many voters felt that Obama was the answer to their prayers—as many had felt about FDR in the 1930s. The nation was indeed in need of a great leader. One author wisely stated:

> We may rely on the best of the New Deal, the matter-of-fact bravery of our parents and grandparents showed then, to help us through today's unexpected challenges. But we don't have to repeat New Deal stimulus experiments, because we know they didn't work.[111]

"In 1936, Keynes wrote, 'Practical men, who believe themselves to be quite exempt from any intellectual influence, are usually the slave of some defunct economist.' In 2008, no defunct economist is more prominent than Keynes himself," according to Mankiw.[112] In May 2009, the nation's new president—Barack Obama—seems to be blind to any other path, as he and his Recovery Act have shoved the nation further and further under the waters of despairing debt. If Obama is not careful, the United States will—as its enemies look on or even assist—eventually drown in a watery grave of endless enslavement to debt and creditors.

The above study clearly demonstrates the dangers of ignorance and the devastation which can follow from "misguided" legislation. Politics is often regarded lightly by the American public, but often the issues being endlessly debated are of true national and individual import. They can mean the survival of hundreds of individuals or the survival of a nation and a heritage of freedom and independence. So many have shed their blood so that U.S. citizens might have the opportunity and privilege to live in a nation such as the United States—with the rights to vote, speak out for or against theories and public issues, and work hard to achieve dreams and financial goals. Yet, this independence must be exercised to protect it from those who disregard it by ignoring the dangers facing the nation caused by economic truths or too much government intervention. Independence depends on an unwavering upholding of truth and sound judgment.

# 9

## HEALTH CARE REFORM: A DIAGNOSIS

According to a CBS News Poll, reported March 24, 2010, "nearly two in three Americans said they wanted Republicans to continue challenging parts of the health care reform bill"; yet, on March 25, the well-known reconciliation bill was sent by the U.S. Senate back to the House with only minor changes.[113] On March 30, President Barack Obama signed into law the massive legislation—a piece of legislation much like the Recovery Act in its initial writing and in its financial effect on the nation. Despite the endless hours of argument, debate, presidential pressure, and confusion, few people still truly know or understand the practically countless details of the new law.

Fighting through the obscure language of legal jargon, certain key elements can be identified as causes for great concern. With even a short examination of unbiased facts, one can discover that the health care reform bill—a bill passed against the will of the majority of the American people—is financially risky at best, targets small businesses as well as Medicare patients and the physicians who are willing to treat them, illogically claims to deliver on broad promises, and infringes upon the rights of patients and their doctors. The passage of such legislation should serve as a call to action—an alert to

American citizens of the need for individuals who are willing to utilize their independence in an effort to protect it.

As already noted in the previous chapter, the United States has accumulated a national debt already essentially impossible to repay. As of March 31, 2010, the national debt had grown to over roughly $13,400,750,000,000 and is still increasing at a rate of approximately a million dollars every thirty seconds to one minute.[114] The majority of the most costly provisions of the massive health care reform legislation will not even come into effect for another four to five years.

In November 2009, the Chinese government was reported to have expressed their concerns to Obama regarding the U.S. debt (which was then expected to double during the next ten years) and the potential cost of his plans for health care reform.[115] The CBO, in its final report on March 20, estimated that the health care legislation will cost $940 billion during the next decade, while cutting the deficit $143 billion in the next decade and $1.2 trillion during the following decade.[116] Yet, even an article in the *New York Times* claimed the CBO's final estimate included deceptive "gimmicks."[117] Even just taking the CBO's report at face value should raise "red flags." First, while it is good news that the federal deficit could be cut, less than $145 billion is truly just a "drop in the bucket"—as is $1.2 trillion—as compared to our current national debt. (Too, health care costs are unquestionably not the only areas of government spending likely to increase during the next twenty years.) In addition, adding another trillion to the federal deficit within the next ten years (likely not including that borrowed sum's interest, et cetera, such as was not included the Recovery Act estimates) is highly alarming—when the Recovery Act was estimated to cost the nation as much as $3.27 trillion and when the national debt is rising approximately $60 million every hour or so. Chinese government officials should not be the only ones who are nervous.

In addition, the just-passed health care reform will likely devastate small businesses—so soon after the recent rough economic slump. CNN provided the following summary of the health care legislation on March 22, 2010:

The Congressional Budget Office has estimated that the exchanges [SHOP exchanges, or Small Business Health Options Programs required by law to be established by states] would ease small business insurance costs, albeit only marginally: premiums in the small-group market are forecast to fall between 1% and 4% under the exchanges, while the amount of coverage would rise by up to 3%.

...

* Starting in 2014, businesses with more than 50 employees will be required to either offer healthcare coverage or pay a penalty of $750 a year per full-time worker. The coverage offered will also have to meet minimum benefits—covering both a specific set of services and 60% of employee health costs overall—or else employers will face additional penalties. ... Furthermore, if the House amendments approved Sunday pass the Senate intact under the reconciliation process, some other small business provisions will change:
* Part-time employees would be counted toward the 50-employee minimum on [a] pro-rated basis based on hours worked, bringing more small businesses into the group required to provide coverage.
* The $750-per-employee penalty for not providing insurance would rise to $2,000.[118]

Common sense alone makes the potential damage to small businesses evident from the above information. Yet, additional information makes the reality even clearer. The *Denver Post* reported the version passed by the House

March 21, 2010, also stipulated that employees who do not acquire health care coverage by 2014 will be fined 1% of their income, 2% of their income by 2015, and 2.5% of their income by 2016. Colorado's state director of the National Federation of Independent Business Tony Gagliardi certainly believed the health care reform legislation (the version passed by the House March 22, 2010) would be harmful to small businesses and stated the following:

> This bill will raise, not lower, insurance costs, and it will increase both taxes and the cost of doing business for the very people they said they wanted to help—small businesses. ... We couldn't have been clearer how damaging this bill will be to Colorado's small businesses and the economic recovery of this country.

In Arvada, Colorado, one small business owner, Russell Wright, was so upset by the legislation's passage on March 21 that the next day, he flew the U.S. flag upside down as a "distress signal."[119]

There is no question that a 21% pay cut would cause any employee financial difficulty; in fact, any employee with such a pay cut might have to look for a better-paying job. Through the Medicare system, doctors are paid by the government for the services they render to Medicare patients. As of April 2, 2010, all physicians were set by law to face a 21% cut in reimbursements from the government for treating Medicare patients. Such a cut would mean, for example, that the government would reimburse a doctor only $294.57 for a Medicare patient's colonoscopy—which on average costs $374.20; similarly, "for a typical visit to the doctor's office, the reimbursement would fall to $51.70 from $65.67 for an established patient ...," according to *BusinessWeek* magazine.[120] On May 28, 2010, Congress allowed the (specifically 21.3%)

cut in reimbursements to become effective June 1.[121] While the costs of health care have been rising in the past several years, this is generally not physicians' fault. As stated by one doctor, Dr. John House, "It is unfair to cut the Medicare payment to physicians because the cost of all areas of medicine is increasing. This increase is a result of better technology, better drugs and longer life spans."[122] In fact, another doctor, Mark Sklar (an endocrinologist in Washington, D.C.), explains the following:

> You may find this hard to believe, but when I first started practicing medicine in 1990 I received more payment for an office visit than I am currently receiving. This has occurred despite the increasing cost of practicing medicine, which is the result of rising malpractice premiums, rents, staff salaries, professional membership fees, license fees, and costs needed to comply with various new regulations. What other profession has experienced a reduction in reimbursement over the last 20 years?[123]

To best treat people, those wishing to become doctors must endure grueling training, endless hours of study, and high costs for excellent educations. Many medical students are driven to endure the education and costs to become the best doctors possible, so they can help others. Congress is punishing all doctors for a problem they did not cause.

Yet, doctors are not the only ones who will suffer from this reimbursement cut. As Dr. House says, "We don't want to stop seeing Medicare patients but we will if Congress leaves us no other option." Dr. House explains that in reality, doctors' practices are "essentially small businesses" with the same financial concerns as other businesses, including staff salaries, office materials, and other bills; if forced into unworkable reimbursement situations, these doctors will have to keep their businesses afloat by cutting the number of Medicare patients seen or the time spent with each patient—or by increasing the costs for all non-Medicare patients.[124] A law intended to reduce health care costs potentially resulting in higher costs for everyone can be described no other way than as a mistake or failure. Higher costs charged by doctors could cause families—who could afford sufficient health care services before—to no longer be able to afford to see their doctor or find good services (also resulting in doctors' losing patients, further adding to their vulnerability as small businesses). It also is easy to see that doctors could have to cut staffers' salaries or even their jobs, resulting in additional economic troubles (including higher unemployment). A number of older doctors might even choose to retire sooner than they had originally planned, or others might find it is simply no longer financially feasible to practice medicine where they are located—forcing them to move (at best) and resulting in poorer care for the patients in that community. Regardless, Medicare patients are most likely to suffer the most from this reimbursement cut to doctors, as a number of doctors will likely simply be unable to afford to risk all the potential financial losses by seeing Medicare patients.

Dr. Sklar also says:

I feel strongly that if doctors are reimbursed more for office visits, they will spend more time with patients. This will lead to fewer referrals by primary-care physicians and result in lower health-care expenditures. Currently, harried primary-care physicians don't have the time to delve into medical problems with a hint of complexity. So patients who could be dealt with if more time was available are referred to specialists or expensive radiology studies.[125]

Yet, Congress has passed legislation which accomplishes the

exact opposite—cutting government reimbursement to physicians. A nameless blogger wrote the following response on March 22, 2010, to a *Reuters* article about the effects of the health care reform legislation on Medicare patients:

> *Reuters* needs to mention that the cardiologists will receive a 42% reduction in reimbursements for Medicare services rendered. Which means, some of these doctors will either retire, or, display a banner "medicare not accepted for payments—cash only please."[126]

According to the American Medical Association (AMA), "'Our message to the U.S. Senate is stop playing games with Medicare patients and the physicians who care for them,' said AMA President J. James Rohack, M.D. 'It is shocking that the Senate would abandon our most vulnerable patients, making them the collateral damage of their procedural games.'"[127]

"In the perfect world, every adult would have a spouse, a house, two children, a dog, and a white picket fence." Similar statements have been used to mock the promises of politicians for decades. Yet, there is some truth both to the logical fallacy intended to be revealed by those statements and to the claim itself. Only in a perfect world will everyone have everything he or she wants. Yet, such a world is impossible. Referring to the previously used example, a drug addict is only happy if given drugs; yet, the addict would likely also want to drive. But the chances are that if the addict did so, he might cause an accident and kill someone. While some ideas have noble intentions (such as ensuring that literally every person who wants a job has one), they are just simply impossible because of the reality of life.

The following is Obama's stated promise (or hope) regarding health care according to the White House's website: "Health reform will make health care more affordable, make health insurers more accountable, expand health coverage to all Americans, and make the health system sustainable, stabilizing family budgets, the Federal budget, and the economy ...."[128] Yet, as seen above, small businesses will likely go bankrupt or have to cut jobs, leading to at least temporarily higher unemployment for those communities and decreased variety of products and services for Americans in general. Small business owners will be essentially punished for their entrepreneurship, and their families will suffer (their children might not even be able to afford to attend college, increasing their chances of someday being unemployed or living near or below poverty level). Medicare patients will likely find that more doctors than before are not just unwilling, but literally unable, to afford to treat them. Likely, many physicians will just choose to take an early retirement or will be forced to work in a different field because they cannot afford to work under the government's demands. This will likely discourage many college students from choosing the field of medicine, further decreasing the number of good doctors and nurses in the United States.

Obama's promise sounds excellent; his idea of making it more possible for every person to be able to have good health care is truly wonderful. Sadly, the legislation now in effect not only fails to deliver on all his promises but even delivers the opposite effects in many regards. Obama and his Democratic supporters would likely argue that given time, they could come closer to fulfilling those grand promises. Sadly, that too is highly unlikely. For example, as discussed in another study, regardless of the good intentions behind minimum wages often advocated by Democrats, the economic reality is that "while minimum wages can greatly improve the lives of those who receive them, it also discourages firms from hiring as many individuals for lower-paying positions. [. . .] Therefore, since minorities are more likely to be affected by minimum-wage laws and the most in need of welfare, Democrats' pressure to raise the minimum-wage damages the lives of minorities by decreasing the number of jobs available to them and forcing more to become dependent on welfare."[129] Similarly, it appears Democrats are currently ignoring economic truths regarding the issue of health care—illogically claiming the recently passed legislation will deliver on Obama's promises.

In October 2009, physician and former Senate Majority Leader Bill Frist published his book *A Heart to Serve*. In the following from his book, Frist explains what he feels are elements necessary in any reform of the healthcare system:

> For me, a twenty-first-century American health-care system should be *patient-centered, consumer-driven,* and *provider-friendly. Patient-centered,* in that the well-being and needs of individuals must be at the heart of every decision we make. *Consumer-driven,* in that individuals should make decisions that drive value and quality. Those who receive care should retain the ultimate control and authority over their treatments, rather than ceding that control to government bureaucrats, insurance companies, or professional organizations that may have their own agendas. And *provider-friendly,* in that the system must make medical professions for nurses and doctors rewarding and fulfilling, limiting the impact of problems like excessive paperwork, intrusive regulation, and out-of-control malpractice suits that too often drive good people away.[130]

It is easy to see the recently enacted health care reform does not fit the bill, as prescribed by U.S. Senator and doctor Bill Frist.

When asked, "Isn't adding 30 million uninsured potential patients to the insurance roles [sic] a patient-centered health care bill?" Congressman and physician Tom Price of Georgia replied:

> It depends on what you're giving them. If you're giving them a card that says you have the right to get in line and wait, that's not patient-centered. If you're giving them a plan that is a substandard plan because of rationing of care and doesn't allow you to get the care that you want to receive for you and your family, that's not patient-centered. If you're dictating to the patients what doctors they're able to see and what procedures and tests they're able to have, that's not patient-centered. So it depends what you're giving them. The fact of the matter is, these bills, the bills passed yesterday, will not improve quality in this nation, they will decrease quality. They won't decrease costs of health care in this nation, they will increase costs. They will not increase access in this nation, they will decease [sic] access in this nation. They will not increase responsiveness of this system; they will decrease the responsiveness of this system. It will destroy innovation that has given us the greatest health care system in the world [see the Appendix for an explanation of this claim] and it will remove choices for the American people. So none of the principles that we hold dear as it relates to health care are improved by what is in these bills.[131]

The idea of excellent health care for all is, again, inspiring. Yet, with a federal budget already so deeply in the red, clearly, Obama's promises could not become a reality without someone having to suffer. The recently passed reform is set to essentially backfire—with Medicare patients having fewer doctors, fewer doctors being able to afford the governments' new demands, and families facing higher costs due to taxes and the Medicare reimbursement cuts. These and many other problems not thoroughly addressed in this book make it clear that no matter how noble or worthy an idea sounds, independently thinking citizens must refuse to automatically trust the accuracy or reality of a person's claims and instead study the facts for themselves. Many U.S. citizens did express their concerns regarding the facts, rather than just the intentions or claims, of the health care reform legislation for many months. Thousands voiced their opposition, yet Congress passed the legislation against the will of the majority of the people. As described by Congressman Price, "The bills that were passed yesterday on the floor of the House of Representatives do not respect individuals. They put their trust in government and not people."[132] Rather than becoming discouraged, U.S. citizens must become more resolved than ever to protect their rights, including their rights as patients and doctors and nurses and college students interested in the field of medicine.

An excellent summary of the concerns which arise from the recently enacted health care reform laws is provided by a well-known and highly respected endocrinologist in Memphis, Tennessee, Dr. Ralph Goodman.[133] While Dr. Goodman approves of the abolition of insurance companies' exclusion of individuals with preexisting conditions and the idea of every individual having health care, he expresses a number of concerns regarding the health care reform legislation in the following responses during an interview:

I do believe everyone should have access to health care. The positives of the new law are that it eliminates exclusion for preexisting conditions and will allow or require everyone to have health care. The people that have not had care prior or have had difficulty getting or affording a policy before will therefore benefit. However no one know[s] what the cost will be, and we may all end up paying more for our policies than we now are. It also requires everyone to buy health insurance or be fined, and I am not sure this is constitutional. I think some physicians may be resentful of the program, not for financial reasons, but for reasons of lack of decision making, and may end up quitting or retiring early, and some of the best candidates to be physicians may be discouraged by the bureaucratic aspects of the system.

So access may end up being less due to fewer qualified MDs. It appears most physicians in private practice are opposed, but most in academics, who live in an "ivory tower," are in favor of the system. It will not change their world at all. The law will definitely infringe on rights. Patient medical information may be open to government scrutiny, and may be passable from one government agency to another. If this ends up resembling the VA hospital, physicians will be constrained to using a certain number of mainly inexpensive and possibly inferior generic drugs, and there may be guidelines on how aggressively we can treat certain conditions based on patient's age and other factors, calculated as the "value" of their life or their life expectancy. For now I do not plan to change anything, but if the system becomes unduly intrusive, I will likely look for other employment. I foresee restrictions on treatment paradigms and available medications and therapies based on what the government thinks is appropriate or within their budget.

It is unfortunate that this bill was passed despite the majority of Americans not approving of it. I also suspect that many of those in favor don't know what is really involved here, and were just following the herd instinct in approving of it. It appears that our elected representatives often disregard our desires and do not truly represent our wishes, instead voting for what they think is best for us, assuming we are too ill-informed or stupid to make a reasonable choice. Citizens should definitely remain vigilant and remove anyone who does not represent their interests.

It seems Congressman Tom Price would concur: "The battle of ideas never ends and the price of liberty is eternal vigilance... And we'll be eternally vigilant."[134]

As of April 2010, measures were being taken and considered by state governments to challenge the health care reform legislation in the Supreme Court. Republicans were promising to work to repeal the legislation. Physicians in politics—Congressman Price and Senator Frist—have practical knowledge and suggestions regarding how to truly address the problems with the U.S. health care system (see the Appendix for Congressman Price's explanation of health care cost causes). What can citizens do to protect themselves and their futures? Independence is never defended by passivity; action must be taken by those who wish to preserve their freedoms. As mentioned earlier, Joseph Galloway wisely stated so many years ago, "For under it [the United States' system of government] no law can be binding on America, to which the people, by their Representatives, have not previously given their consent: this is the essence of liberty, and what more would her people desire?"[135] When "their Representatives" refuse to listen to the people, it is time for the people to ensure they have representatives who will listen—especially since, as already discussed, the representatives actually receive their power from the people.

# PART III:
## THE DEFENSE OF INDEPENDENCE

*The most important political office is that of the private
citizen. – Supreme Court Justice Louis D. Brandeis*[136]

# 10

## TAKE NOTE OF THE VOTE

"Well, I don't vote because my vote doesn't count." If every political activist received a nickel for each time he or she heard that statement, political activists would be a very wealthy group. It is commonly believed that one vote does not make much difference. While it is true that one out of millions is not mathematically much, it is also true that one's vote should be more so viewed as a cup of milk—that is half full, rather than half empty. The impact of one vote can be tremendous, in many situations—but the greatest difference is when one person understands the value of his vote, as does another...and another...and another... If every citizen ceased to believe in the value of his or her vote, no one would vote. The reverse is also true—if every citizen did believe in the value of his or her vote, the wishes of the nation would be more accurately represented. In fact, there might be fewer complaints if everyone truly had a say in governmental affairs. Yet, all citizens do have that opportunity for a say in their government—if they would only grasp it.

"No taxation without representation" was a major war cry for the colonists prior to the American Revolution. Despite their citizenship with Great Britain, they were being taxed—without having representatives to speak for or against the taxes upon the colonists. Blood was shed for the belief in the people's voice being heard in government…and for the conviction that governing authorities should receive their authority from the people. Throughout history, countless men and women have lost their lives in battle to preserve or fight for their children's privilege to vote.

Many try to claim that the Electoral College that selects the president is outdated and needs revision, while others insist on acknowledging the wisdom behind the design of the system (understanding that any manmade system will be flawed). It was rooted in compromise, as can be seen by a detailed study of the Electoral College and its origination. The signers of the Constitution believed the members of the Electoral College would be selected by people who knew them and trusted them; they believed the members would know leaders capable of leading the country and did not foresee such a large nation coming into existence. Yet, the Founders also believed in avoiding discrimination of small states, which did result in the system's disproportionate weighting of votes. Yet, no one has yet been able to invent an unquestionably better system…and even a study of reality reveals that truly every vote does count.

For example, how have forty-four Presidents of the United States been elected? Each has been elected by the casting of one vote at a time by millions of concerned citizens. As was especially clear with the recall of a number of Toyota's cars in early 2010 due to one small (in size) part, merely because something is large and made up of small parts does not mean that the small parts are unimportant. The United States is a large nation of millions and millions of citizens. The president is to serve as essentially a representative of all those millions of people, such as when dealing with the leaders of other nations. The president is elected by these people whom he or she represents…by their votes. It is a complex system—which functions best with all its parts present and operating properly (as does a car). The faulty gas pedals on Toyota's recalled cars were small pieces, especially as compared to the whole; but any car's gas pedal is critical, despite its size. Every vote is important. Every vote works together to result in the election of a candidate to the presidency—and to every other political office, such as mayor or sheriff or governor.

In April of 2009, a special election for the New York 20th congressional district was held. Once the votes had been counted, it was discovered that the Democratic candidate received 77,725 votes; the Republican also received 77,725 votes. CBS News predicted the fate of the candidates would fall into the hands of the absentee voters.[137] What a huge difference those absentee voters' ballots made. Each vote counted—even those in the 77,725 cast for each candidate. Though a simplistic comparison, voting is similar to a mathematical equation—as alluded to above. Four is often represented as two plus two; yet, four is also four ones. In other words, though one is smaller than two, it still can add up to something larger. Again, though each citizen's vote is just one out of many, all those "ones" add up to a total that changes the course of history. Why would not someone want to be one of those "ones"?

Another common belief of U.S. citizens which is kin to the belief already disproved is that there is no need to try to make a difference. Many citizens—often those unhappy with the state of affairs—possess an almost resigned attitude that accepts or surrenders to the imperfections and flaws of the U.S. government and causes apathy (discussed more in an earlier chapter). Citizens often feel that politics and government is a hopeless cause; yet such is not true.

The following is a true story about an anonymous widow, who lived alone in her home of almost forty years and suffered from a leg ailment her doctors could not explain or cure.

She had spent her over seventy years living a "clean," mostly happy life; she had never smoked, taken drugs, or participated in other such activities that plagued the younger generations. Her children and grandchildren lived far away—even in other states. One evening, she suddenly had an attack of kidney stones. But the X-ray in the emergency room showed more than just kidney stones. It showed terminal, untreatable lung cancer. How did she contract lung cancer? She had never even held a cigarette. Yet, her brothers had during her childhood. Her brothers were heavy smokers.

Smoking has been proven beyond the shadow of a doubt to be harmful. Obviously, smoking and exposure to cigarette smoke are not the only causes of lung cancer. But smoking does kill. It does contribute to an astonishing number of deaths. In fact, "nearly 1 of every 5 deaths is related to smoking"—according to the American Cancer Society.[138] Those who drink and drive or take drugs and drive are held responsible for deaths they cause by their habits and reckless behavior. How is smoking any less a deadly habit for which people should be held responsible?

Beginning in 1998, with California's ban on smoking in public places,[139] state legislators across the nation began to recognize the danger of smoking. As of May 21, 2010, "39 states have some type of public smoking bans, with 26 banning smoking in any enclosed public place, while 11 states have no bans at all."[140] Certainly, many—primarily smokers—were frustrated as those laws were passed (as drug and alcohol addicts are likely frustrated with the laws that apply to them), but those laws were passed in efforts by the states to protect their people from a deadly habit of a minority. Many have rightly praised the passage of these laws. The legislators behind the laws were elected by citizens. The citizens' votes counted; they helped to select their state leaders. These state leaders worked together to likely save the lives of thousands. Every vote does count; voting does matter. Who governs can make a huge difference in the lives of citizens; it can be a matter of life and death for some.

It can be a matter of life and death for those not even yet able to speak. There is incredible controversy regarding abortion. What one often hears are arguments regarding when life actually begins. But if one were to honestly examine the issue, even if humans could not actually know exactly when their lives began and when their children's lives began, does it not follow that if there is even potential for life…if there is even that chance of a special, unique person with a soul coming into existence…that annihilating that chance of life is still wrong? Why do farmers plant seeds and nurture them and protect them and become frustrated if birds snatch the seeds from the soil? Not every seed will grow into a fruitful plant, but every seed has that potential of living. If someone were to kill any person walking around today—young or old—it would be considered murder. It is illogical to claim that killing an unborn child is not murder—when every person alive today began as an unborn child. The fact that each has begun as an unborn child—unable to speak or fend for him/herself—does not make each person any less a human or a person. So every unborn child has the likelihood of coming into the world and living as a person. If a woman were pregnant and someone were to murder her (as has certainly happened before), the husband would of course grieve not just the loss of his wife, but of his unborn child as well. Both were individuals—only one was not yet able to survive on its own.

Laws can and have been passed to permit and restrict abortion. The legislators behind these laws vote according to their beliefs about this sensitive topic. The voters behind these legislators vote according to their beliefs about abortion. Those who are "pro-choice" vote with adamancy to ensure their "freedom to choose." Those who are "pro-life" vote to save lives. Just one vote can make the difference, as already discussed. How can someone not want to vote when he or she realizes so much is at stake? Everyone respects those who save a life—through heroic actions of doctoring, rescuing, and the like. Yet, in reality, every U.S. citizen has the opportunity to save a life—with not the bullet, but the ballot. What more motivation to vote can a person want?

Many other just as critical issues could be mentioned, such as gay marriage. Yet, even the two political "footballs" mentioned above are enough to make the reality and urgency of voter participation "hit home." U.S. citizens have been given the opportunity and, thus, the responsibility to vote and use each vote to defend their morals and beliefs and rights—a right of freedom. Casting even one vote can save lives. That is a very simple, easy way to accomplish great good—to even save a life—and one must remember, in the words of the nation's sixth President John Quincy Adams, "Always vote for principle, though you may vote alone, and you may cherish the sweetest reflection that your vote is never lost."[141]

# 11

## Run for the Right Reasons

Voting is not the only action a U.S. citizen can take to make a great impact on the nation and the lives of fellow citizens. One can be an elected official—one of those in whom the people have entrusted their futures and livelihoods and posterity. It is often believed that one has to have huge "war chests" (accumulations of campaign donations) in order to win an election. That is not always true. It depends on the situation and seat sought. Only a few years ago, a state legislator known to this author who had served his people for many years stated he had never once held a fundraiser; he personally walked door-to-door to the homes of the citizens he wanted to represent and earned their support. His was obviously a unique situation—but one which proved that such a simple campaign is not impossible.

If one decides to run for office, the specific rules vary in each state, but in a number of states, a filing fee must be paid (the fee is usually a relatively insignificant amount). For a number of positions, a citizen must file for candidacy with the secretary of state's office. Regardless, contacting the secretary of state's office is a certain, simple way to determine all the requirements for running for office.

To win the people's trust, a candidate must never waver.

He or she must keep promises and must not compromise his or her principles. He must always remain respectful and patient—even when baited by the opposition. Retaining one's dignity and integrity is crucial, and clearly communicating one's compassion and interest in the lives and priorities of the constituents is noted by voters. Each of these cannot be truly accomplished without sincerity. Just as children are taught that dogs can sense fear, voters can sense insincerity. A candidate must truly wish to serve the people. A candidate with greed or a hunger for power might still win an election, but the most deeply respected and admired elected officials are those who humbly view their positions of power as honors bestowed upon them by their constituents whom they represent.

It is truly a great honor to be an elected official—in any capacity. To be selected as the one among hundreds to millions of people to represent the values and interests of the people of the United States is a privilege to be deeply appreciated. To serve under the shadow of revered leaders gone on before is a task not to be taken lightly. To hold such power and ability to make a difference should be viewed as an opportunity to make a great difference for the people, not for oneself; trust is destroyed when the power "goes to an official's head" and he or she begins to seek only what can help him or her.

It is especially difficult not to lose that focus when reelection season nears, especially if one wants the position of power for self. Temptations to compromise in efforts to secure votes and dollars increase. Yet, if one focuses on the trust bestowed upon him or her by the people, if one focuses on the true purpose of his or her position, one will be guided by what is truly best for the people. This will not always guarantee reelection, but it will guarantee the trust and respect of those who first believed in the candidate and elected him or her. It will guarantee that the people will be represented—as first desired by the Founding Fathers—and not merely seen as statistics and votes to buy with insincere promises or flattery.

Almost as critical is that the public can see these qualifies of leadership in the candidate, even if they are not dealing with the candidate one-on-one. The campaign staff has almost as much power over the public's perception of the candidate as the candidate himself does. Whoever answers the phones is especially important. If a potential volunteer or donor calls the campaign headquarters, respect and efficient, courteous "customer service" from whomever answers the phone will go a long way in the caller's mind. Yet, if the staffer who answers treats the caller as a nuisance or aggravation, untold damage could occur. Words alone do not convince a caller that the staffer is pleased to deal with the caller; a caller can easily sense a bad attitude from a staffer.

These rules of etiquette or "customer service" apply to every campaign staffer, including and perhaps especially the campaign manager. Volunteer coordinators must make the volunteers feel special and important—for that is the truth. Volunteerism, particularly in the world of politics, has grown to be more and more rare within the past ten years (at least in certain regions of the country). Dedicated volunteers are more valuable than money or supplies. In business, marketing personnel occasionally make use of those who are sometimes termed opinion leaders; opinion leaders are more trusted by the general public since they are not actually employed by the business but still advocate the product. Volunteers are often opinion leaders in their communities; if they become dedicated to a campaign and candidate, their influence will likely cause other members of the community to consider voting for the candidate and even possibly volunteering for the campaign. If these facts are kept in mind, it should be easy for staffers to treat volunteers with the respect they deserve.

A special note to campaign staffers regards the "older generations." While there are benefits to having volunteers from the "younger generations" (such as those discussed in the later chapter dedicated to college students), it is also important that older volunteers are treated with just as much respect and enthusiasm as the younger ones. In the last few years, there has been a growing trend to ignore or even patronize older volunteers because they are not technically savvy or as energetic as the younger help. Regardless of their skills on the computer and regardless of their physical abilities, many of these older volunteers—especially the "seasoned" ones who have helped with many campaigns of the past—have wisdom that defies all cultural and technological changes. People, as a whole, do not truly change. Many of the rules of the political world are the same as they were decades and even centuries ago. These volunteers can even help advise how to ward off the dangers that come with the new technology-centered world (for example, campaigns can be just as guilty of impersonal communication and organization as large businesses—a common complaint of both the young and old). Staffers should listen to the suggestions of these special volunteers and should at least honor them with the same (or more) respect bestowed upon the younger volunteers.

One might ask how to ensure that staffers will have the discussed qualities, since the candidate cannot keep "tabs" on every staffer every minute of the day. Depending on the campaign's size (varying with the position sought), often a candidate will have little to do with the majority of his campaign staff. But if the candidate carefully picks the campaign manager and specifies what he or she expects from the manager and whomever the manager hires, the staff will likely be composed of quality workers. The manager should be humble and dedicated; he or she should share the opinions of the candidate. There is a growing tendency to hire "career campaign managers"; hiring such a manager can certainly produce good results. Yet, sincere interest in how the candidate is portrayed and whether or not the candidate wins is key and more likely to exist if the manager personally knows the candidate and wishes to serve the candidate. If the manager appreciates the candidate and who the candidate is, the manager will be more cautious to protect the candidate's integrity, more sincere in convincing donors and activists of the candidate's qualities and leadership, and more dedicated to victory.

Just as important are the political directors, communication directors, and even the finance staff (including treasurers, accountants, etc.). The political director is in an especially important position to ensure that key volunteers such as county chairmen are respected and appreciated. Communication directors who deal directly with the media have to possess great patience and great conviction or dedication to the candidate. The finance and accounting staff require an attention to detail that ties to a belief in the candidate. All members of the team must be ethical and respectful of the opposition (at all times) and must pay attention to details. If the accounting staff makes a mistake, it can cause the candidate to appear less than capable at best and deceitful at worst—even if he or she had nothing to do with the accounting error. If those in charge of mail-outs allow typos and other errors to appear, it can again give the voter the impression that the candidate and his team are not truly competent. If anyone in the communications department or the political director "spouts off" about the opposition (even when not at work, but in a public setting), the general public may become aware of the staffer's disrespect and misunderstand the candidate. Honesty on all levels—from the candidate to the receptionist—is critical; once dishonesty creeps into the campaign at any point, it is much easier for deception to become acceptable amongst the entire staff. The candidate and his campaign leadership must set the example and remain firm in their dedication to honest operations.

Perhaps someone feels he has all the qualities and convictions needed to be such a candidate—but is not an experienced speaker and is not keen about the idea of public speaking. Focusing on those for whom the campaign is being run—the voters—can help with that discomfort. If one remembers that he or she is speaking with the purpose of representing the people—focusing on the ideals and beliefs and determination that drove one to decide to run in the first place—speaking in public could become very little different than persuading voters one on one. In fact, that is what the candidate is truly doing. He or she is speaking directly to each individual—regardless of how many individuals are present. Focusing on the purpose of the campaign will help a candidate to realize it is not truly about him/herself; it is about making a difference in the lives of fellow citizens.

If a candidate followed each of the above suggestions, he or she would be independent indeed. Viewing the campaign as an opportunity to selflessly serve rather than grab power, carefully picking likeminded staff, and even speaking with the people in mind—each of these actions are foundational to making the candidate unique and to aptly portraying the sincere devotion of the candidate to the voters and the nation. Candidates all too often fail to follow one or more of the above suggestions. While they sometimes still win, and while they might even serve the public well, many who lose their focus find themselves humiliated and ashamed by their mistakes or the voters' discontentment.

True political leaders are those who view their positions of power as honors and trusts which must be revered; with that perspective, retaining one's integrity, connecting with the voters, and other similar "independent" actions will be easy. What could be a greater way to inspire in others a desire to defend the nation's independence than running for public office, not from a hunger for power but from a humble, sincere desire to serve and lead and protect fellow citizens! The nation needs individuals who are willing to run for office—to fulfill the roles first envisioned by the Framers…as defenders of freedom and independence through their representing the people's best interests.

# 12

## LET SOMEONE ELSE DO IT

Voting and running for office are not the only two activities a U.S. citizen can do to affect the political process. While many citizens feel there is little they can do because of their schedules, limited finances, or other reasons, in reality, the political process would grind to a halt without citizens who are active in "small" ways. Politics and government do compose a complex world, but actions which take even five minutes can make a huge difference.

"I do not have time to volunteer" is a common claim of many, and it is true that the majority of U.S. citizens do not have time to volunteer for a political campaign, which makes those who do have the time exceptionally valuable. Yet, perhaps if more citizens understood how much—or how little—they could do while still greatly helping campaigns, more citizens would invest even short lengths of time in helping a candidate become their elected leader. Technological advances make volunteer work from home possible; with Internet services such as MapQuest and others, volunteers can easily follow customized maps to deliver signs or other materials to campaign supporters' doors. There are hundreds of options and opportunities for U.S. citizens—and even just one or two hours of a volunteer's time during the course of an entire campaign can be a huge help to candidates.

Few citizens have been a part of a parade—such as one for the Fourth of July. A fun, easy way to be involved in a parade is to join a campaign team. Campaigns often have "floats" in patriotic parades and will sometimes recruit practically a small army of volunteers to walk behind the "float" (usually a car decorated with campaign signs, stickers, flags, etc.) along the parade route. Sometimes candidates walk the parade lines themselves, shaking hands and meeting people; candidates need volunteers to follow up with those people and catch ones the candidates missed, distributing stickers and litera- ture. Door-to-door walks with small teams of volunteers and campaign staff are also commonly used in political campaigns. Door-to-door walks would be a perfect way to accomplish great good for fellow citizens and improve one's health.

Perhaps walking is not someone's interest or is not a very practical option. There are plenty of indoor campaign needs as well. Yard signs need to be constructed. Some signs are designed such that they only need to be slipped onto metal stands; others need stapling. Letters asking for donations or other such mail need to be folded, stuffed into envelopes, sealed, and stamped. Sometimes campaigns need volunteers to enter names and contact information of volunteers and donors into the database system on computers.

A huge component of any campaign strategy is telephone work. If someone enjoys talking on the telephone, this is the job for him or her. While some dislike telephone work because they are calling strangers, a different outlook on such tasks is that talking with voters on the telephone is a chance to meet dozens or even hundreds of people. It is a chance to reach the lives of people someone would otherwise never have a chance to meet. Call lists can be completed at the headquarters or at a person's home (the list can be picked up at the headquarters or emailed to the volunteer). In some situations, even thirty minutes a week can be a great help. There are all types of call lists. There are call lists compiled to target voters in "get out the vote" efforts; there are call lists to arrange for delivery of signs and materials; there are even call lists to notify existing volunteers of an upcoming event. These types and others have their own unique experiences.

The key to all of these volunteer activities is the enjoyment one can have in socializing while volunteering. The camaraderie amongst dedicated volunteers and staff can be very special. There is something rare and honorable about a person who is willing to do such work for a cause without pay; staffers and candidates know this and are deeply grateful to volunteers. Volunteers all share a common goal and purpose—which can make discussions over mail-outs lively and interesting, as they compare notes over the latest news or the last campaign event. Voters who answer their phones when a volunteer calls can become new friends or new volunteers; sometimes these voters will express their gratitude to the volunteer for the volunteer's hard work. The "bottom line" is that volunteers share a special understanding or bond. They not only have a candidate or set of ideals in common, but they also share a unique dedication to their nation—to the idea of making a difference in the lives of countless fellow citizens…through their acts of volunteerism in defense of their freedoms and heritage.

A perfect example of the importance and the rewards of volunteerism is that of the volunteers for former Speaker of the House Newt Gingrich. Marjorie Crayton came to the United States as a British citizen with her husband (an American soldier) in 1959; both Marjorie and her husband shared a deep interest in politics and history for years, even prior to their coming to the United States. Following her husband's death in 1992, her son-in-law (whom she had encouraged to become interested in politics and government) arranged for Marjorie to begin volunteering for Newt Gingrich's campaign. The first day she worked in Gingrich's office, she met several people who she recalls would become "my dearest friends." Marjorie says, "I just came to love it [volunteering]"; although she originally had arranged to volunteer only a couple hours a couple times a week, she began to come into the office each day. She would arrive even before the campaign staffers, who eventually gave her a key to the headquarters, so she could open the office. After time, she was assigned the task of co-ordinating all Gingrich's volunteers. Marjorie remembers the majority of volunteers were individuals who wanted to help Gingrich because "he had helped them somewhere along the way with problems they had had. … It was their way to pay him back. They told me there was no way they could pay him back monetarily, so they … spent long hours in order to repay him for the wonderful things he had done for them." Marjorie describes, "We all became great friends. … A lot of them were retired by now; we had teachers, business people, … husbands and wives, and single people. We would sit around the table, stuffing envelopes, putting stamps on, and all other kinds of things…we would talk about the events of the day, current events, things happening in the world …. We all had a common thing …." Marjorie felt volunteering was important because of loving history and "trying to preserve what was good in this country [..., and] our Constitution"; she also explains that while "I was proud to be an English person (and I am still proud I was born there), finally I did consent to become a [U.S.] citizen; and of course, I am very, very proud to be a citizen." Even once Newt Gingrich left office, Marjorie and many of her friends continued to work on other campaigns, including ones for state offices, governor, Congress, and President of the United States. According to

Marjorie, for her, volunteering "was almost a full time job... but I loved it...oh, I just loved every minute of it."[142]

One couple who became friends with Marjorie—Fred and Pat Allen—of Marietta, Georgia, have also understood the great frontline of defense of volunteerism and have worked for various political campaigns and entities over the past forty to forty-five years. Pat worked for Newt Gingrich two to three days a week for six years (until his resignation); the couple has worked diligently on campaigns for such positions as county commissioner, state legislator, governor, Congress, and President of the United States. Fred and Pat have served on their local GOP county committee and have attended state party conventions as delegates for their county. Fred, as of March 2010, served as a vice GOP chair for his district. Not every candidate for whom they have worked has won the election, but Fred and Pat have never lost sight of why they chose to be volunteers. Their hard work and dedication have inspired countless candidates and citizens—both young and old. In 2005, at the Georgia GOP state convention, their tireless efforts were recognized as they were both awarded the Volunteer of the Year award. Money, fame, nor power were Fred and Pat's objectives as they sacrificed their time and energy to work behind candidates and political leaders. Their advice to others, especially younger citizens, is "to get involved and support in a direct manner someone who shares your beliefs" and "to vote and shape the agenda towards protecting the ideas that formed our republic and that will provide an honest and valued future for the generations that follow—your children and grandchildren." These convictions are what have motivated Fred and Pat Allen for over four decades. Fred and Pat understand the inestimable value of the independence Americans have as U.S. citizens, as evidenced in their response when asked for an interview:

Don't make it sound like we are any different than many millions of others in this great country called America— proven to be the most successful experiment the world has known in the value of the individual and the freedom to live and work for the benefit of self and the country overall.[143]

Key players in the Revolutionary War were called Minutemen. These soldiers and others were volunteers who joined the cause not for payment or glory; they were ready at any minute to fight the British...to defend themselves, their families, and their rights. With so many serious issues currently in debate— with the very nature and fabric and future of the nation at stake—"Minutemen" are needed now more than ever in recent decades. The nation needs citizens who are willing to stand up and make their voices heard through the ballot; the nation needs citizens who will take on a responsibility that few others will accept and who will urge family, friends, and neighbors to do the same. The United States needs more citizens like Marjorie Crayton and Fred and Pat Allen—citizens who are special in their undying devotion to protect and defend their freedoms and independence through even small sacrifices of time and energy.

A fictional obituary (once heard by this author) was written anonymously regarding churches and their members; but with a few adaptations, it makes a valid point for U.S. citizens as well.

I know that all of you were saddened to learn this week of the death of one of our community's most valuable members -- Someone Else.

Someone's passing created a vacancy that will be difficult to fill. Else has been a member of the community for many years, and for every one of those years, Someone did far more than the average citizen's share of the work. Whenever leadership was mentioned, this wonderful person was looked to for inspiration as well as results. "Someone Else can work with that project or campaign." Whenever there was a job to do, an event to organize, voters and volunteers to recruit, or a meeting to attend, one name was on everyone's lips, "Let Someone Else do it."

Someone Else was a wonderful person, sometimes appearing super-human, but one citizen can only do so much. Were the truth known, everyone expected too much of Someone Else. Now Someone Else is gone. We wonder what we are going to do. Someone Else left a wonderful example to follow, but who is going to follow it? Who is going to do the things Someone Else did? Remember, we can't depend on Someone Else anymore.

The truth is that U.S. citizens cannot rely on "someone else" to do the responsibilities all citizens share as citizens. If everyone were to always depend on "someone else," the United States would cease to be the nation of "We the People" it was designed to be.

# 13

## SPECIAL CONSIDERATIONS FOR COLLEGE STUDENTS

Invincible, endlessly energetic, and eager for chances to advance one's future career—the American college student is the perfect asset for a political campaign. Although students have studies to consider, campaigns can use the energy and vision of these members of the "younger generations." Landing key low-level positions on campaigns and even volunteering is hugely advantageous to students; such activities are impressive on the resumes of students interested in politics and government. In reality, most organizations of any type are impressed with volunteerism.

College students are especially helpful to campaigns because students do not have the same type of "attachments" and responsibilities as older adults. College students usually have no mouths to feed and no spouse to return home to. The last seventy-two hours of a campaign are especially critical and require manual labor (such as holding signs at street corners) at difficult times, such as the dinner hour. College students often have both the energy and the time or flexibility desperately needed by campaigns. Sometimes, campaigns are even able to pay a small sum to those volunteers who work exceptionally hard during the campaign. For example, in 2004, a number of volunteers for the Seventy-Two Hour Task Force for Georgia's Republican Victory Center received checks of $50 after victory had been realized on Election Day. For college students, fifty dollars can be a significant portion of an important textbook or enough gas to drive home. In some situations, professors (especially those teaching political courses) might even be willing to extend extra credit for volunteerism.

Internships with campaigns or government offices can be hugely helpful to both "parties." The campaign benefits from the special characteristics of the college student, and the college student gains great experience, earns another admirable opportunity to list on his or her resume, sometimes simultaneously earns college credit, and even occasionally earns extra cash as well. This provides special opportunities for the student's university as well. Universities may choose to advertise their flexibility and willingness to work with students regarding internship opportunities, and such situations can prove beneficial to the universities if their students help candidates win seats in state legislatures or Congress. In reality, internships and other similar work-study situations create a "win-win" situation for everyone involved.

Working in some way for campaigns is not the only option available to college students. If a student has an interest in writing, the student should investigate whether or not the university (or local) newspaper would be willing to include another editorial writer. Students could even routinely submit letters to the editor, if the newspaper permits such letters. Just talking to friends and encouraging them to become activists and to understand their government can bring about quiet, but great, results. Although college friends may not always stay in touch, they are rarely forgotten. If friends can see that a student is truly dedicated to serving his or her country, they will remember that student's commitment—perhaps for the rest of their lives. Even if they are not inspired to action while in college, that one student's example may spur action decades later.

Another related opportunity is to find political groups or clubs on campus. There are national organizations for both College Republicans and College Democrats. Club leadership can organize campus events, such as debates, workshops, and games. These events could even encourage university faculty and staff to become more involved—which can then create a community effort, as the faculty and staff then tell their friends and neighbors of their activities. Clubs can host important speakers (such as state legislators, congressional members, national and state party leadership, etc.), broadcast its message through the selling of t-shirts, distribute literature, and other similar activities. The possibilities are truly limitless, especially if one is at a large or well-known university or one located in a large city.

Key to college students' true success in helping campaigns are traits needed in candidates and other activists. College students need to possess a humility and desire to serve, rather than a hunger for power; they need a true respect of the candidate, staffers, and older volunteers—from whom they can learn much—as well as a deep appreciation and love for their country and freedoms. Becoming an activist at an early age is a special opportunity for college students (and, in reality, even younger individuals); it is a chance to develop leadership skills and knowledge which will prove highly beneficial in years to come, when it comes time for the student to become the staffer, the candidate, or even the retired volunteer. Even though it is said often and in varying situations, the saying "the future rests in the hands of young people" should be a motivating truth to college students, as they realize the responsibility and privilege which lies ahead for them. Defending one's independence can become a lifelong commitment—as

111

one grasps the chance to truly shape history and the future of the nation.

CONCLUSION

# INHERITANCE OF INDEPENDENCE

Every citizen of the United States of America has an inheritance—an invaluable inheritance bought with the blood of countless courageous men and women who—over the course of history—were willing to give everything, so their posterity could remain free and have the independence they themselves enjoyed and treasured. They wanted future generations to have those great opportunities of independence—the liberty to think and choose for oneself, the privilege to vote and voice opinions, and the form of limited government which they knew equals liberty.

There have been many thousands of individuals who never shot a bullet on the battlefield but instead sacrificed their time and energy to author books of inspiring patriotism or wisdom. There have been even more who have spoken out in dedication to justice and freedom and in defiance of injustice and tyranny—to friends, neighbors, and family or through the legal right provided them with the ballot. Others through history have been willing to sacrifice money and time while running for office or helping great candidate leaders realize their potential.

The United States of America is unquestionably the greatest nation in existence today and the greatest in history—because of her endless opportunities made possible by the uniquely protected form of independence...invented by a group of wise men who learned history's lessons and believed in the value of independent thinking. These individuals' independent thinking created a special government with multiple protections against tyranny built into the system and a nation in which other independent thinkers would have a chance to make their voices heard or put their views into practice in inventions, books, or speeches.

All these leaders of history—famous and hardly known—demonstrated their great self-sufficiency as they respected the wisdom of the past and formed opinions regarding the present. The result is a challenge to U.S. citizens today to continue this legacy, this heritage of freedom—to fight any threats to freedom and pass on to future generations this inheritance... an inheritance sought during history as much as gold or any other riches. The question today is who will take up this challenge? Will apathy and ignorance take the helm of the future of the United States?

As was seen in Massachusetts in early 2010, independent thinking can make a difference. It can defy all predictions or expectations, as U.S. citizens take their futures into their own hands with the special rights given them. There has recently been a renewed interest in independence—a renewed understanding of the vital role of independence in U.S. citizens' lives—as the federal government has become more and more intrusive and less and less responsive to "We, the People," from whom the federal government has received its power. According to Supreme Court Justice Louis D. Brandeis,

Those who won our independence believed that the final end of the state was to make men free to develop their faculties .... They valued liberty both as an end and as a means. They believed liberty to be the secret of happiness and courage to be the secret of liberty.[144]

"Life, liberty, and the pursuit of happiness" was the main drive behind the author and the signers of the Declaration of Independence. Such is the essence of independence and was believed then to be the inherent right of every human—all created equal by God. Thus, the government is the "creature" of the people, rather than the people the creatures or subjects to be under the complete control of the government. U.S. citizens must never lose sight of this truth, or else they will lose their declared independence of over two centuries.

Knowledge of law and current threats and a resolve to actively protect one's inheritance are the surest defenses to the threats which face the heritage and fabric of the United States of America. As Founding Father Samuel Adams once said,

The liberties of our country, the freedom of our civil Constitution, are worth defending at all hazards; and it is our duty to defend them against all attacks. We have received them as a fair inheritance from our worthy ancestors: they purchased them for us with toil and danger and expense of treasure and blood, and transmitted them to us with care and diligence. It will bring an everlasting mark of infamy on the present generation, enlightened as it is, if we should suffer them to be wrested from us by violence without a struggle, or to be cheated out of them by the artifices of false and designing men.[145]

Never will anything be defended by every person believing "someone else" will fight the threats. John Quincy Adams

115

believed,

> Individual liberty is individual power, and as the power of
> a community is a mass compounded of individual powers,
> the nation which enjoys the most freedom must neces-
> sarily be in proportion to its numbers the most powerful
> nation.[146]

Independence is dependent on individuals. There is no power
greater than independent individuals determined to defend
their liberties—and that will result in a strong United States
of America...and an unending inheritance of independence.

# APPENDIX

Congressman Tom Price explains his claim that the U.S. has the best health care system in the world in the following excerpt of an interview conducted on March 22, 2010:

The fact of the matter is if you look at disease specific criteria, the United States has the greatest health system in the world. If you have a heart attack today, the likelihood of you surviving that heart attack is better where you're seated than anywhere else in the world. ... One of [the] things that the World Health Organization uses as one of their items that they put into that equation is whether or not you're insured. Well, in this nation, oftentimes whether or not you are insured doesn't have anything to do with whether or not you get treatment. In fact, there are people everyday [sic] who are treated by the generosity and altruism of the physicians providing care across this land who have no insurance whatsoever. The World Health Organization doesn't count that at all. So when individuals who are of means in France get really sick, where do they go? They go to the United States.[147]

Congressman Price describes causes of rising health care in the following excerpt of the same interview:

This [the health care reform legislation passed March 21] is a move into a major intervention of the federal government into every aspect and principle of health care that Americans hold dear…in the wrong direction. Whether it's the quality, whether it's the access, whether its the affordability or the choices Americans desire and demand—none of them are improved by this legislation. The status quo however is unacceptable. There are positive solutions that we ought to be addressing. The fact this bill doesn't address any costs at all in a positive way is very troubling… Because the way this bill addresses costs is to have the government dictate to people what they must do… The way that we believe costs ought to be addressed is to address the cost drivers in health care. They're forming drivers of cost in health care. Taxation… we ought to decrease taxes on those providing care…decrease taxation on all Americans, frankly. Regulation… the regulatory oppression in health care is huge. Not just in the doctor's office, but in every single laboratory and every single medical facility in this nation, every single hospital. And that regulatory oppression makes it much more difficult for care to be provided. And then litigation. There is nothing in these bills that addresses the lawsuit abuse in health care right now. And that drives probably 25, 20-25% of every single health care dollar in this nation. And then, finally, competition. This decreases competition, not increases competition. And competition right now in health care is markedly limited. So things like purchasing your health insurance across state lines or being able to pool with other Americans to be able to get the purchasing power of millions, so that you actually do interject some competition into the system. Those things will drive down the cost of health care because they work by individuals selecting what they want for themselves... not what the government wants for them.[148]

# ACKNOWLEDGEMENTS

I will forever be grateful to Dr. Sam Hester of Hester Publications and Freed-Hardeman University, who so kindly asked me to write this book and helped make my dream come true; thanks too to Matt Neely, Dr. Hester's expert printer. Stephen H. Morris, J.D., of Freed-Hardeman University is to be especially thanked for all his instruction in government and law, as reflected in this book. Deserving of thanks as well are Margaret Payne, who graciously edited this book, and Karen S. Garvin, who also kindly used her expertise to edit certain portions of this book.

A special note of thanks is due to Fred and Pat Allen, Marjorie Crayton, and the other members of the "Newt Group," including Lou Murphy and others who have passed on. Much of the knowledge contained in this book was imparted to me by these special people, and even more information was due to the learning made possible by the wonderful experiences these individuals helped bring about with their guidance and unending encouragement.

A special note of thanks is also due to Dr. Ralph Goodman—who likely saved my mother's life and has shown an endless willingness to help my entire family and a compassion for all his patients; to my many friends who have encouraged me as I wrote this book; and to many other great individuals—such as President George W. Bush; Senators Bill Frist, Lamar Alexander, and Bob Corker; Congressman Tom Price; and Governor and First Lady Perdue—who have had such a great impact on my life and the lives of countless others.

# NOTES

[1] "State of the Union with John King" and "Transcripts," CNN, January 24, 2010, http://archives.cnn.com/TRANSCRIPTS/1001/24/sotu.03.html (accessed April 14, 2010).

[2] Associated Press, "Obama Asks 2008 Supporters to Help in 2010," CBSNews.com, April 26, 2010, http://www.cbsnews.com/stories/2010/04/26/politics/main6434253.shtml (accessed June 16, 2010).

[3] George Hewes, "Eyewitness Account by George Hewes," Boston Tea Party Historical Society, http://www.boston-tea-party.org/account-george-hewes.html (accessed April 15, 2010).

[4] Library of Congress, "The American Revolution 1774–1783" and "The Thomas Jefferson Papers—1743 to 1827 Timeline," American Memory Collection, http://memory.loc.gov/ammem/collections/jefferson_papers/mtjtime2a.html (accessed April, 15, 2010).

[5] Thomas Kindig, "Short Biographies on Each of the 56 Declaration Signers" and "Signers of the Declaration of Independence," Independence Hall Association, http://www.ushistory.org/declaration/signers/index.htm (accessed April 14, 2010).

[6] Benjamin Franklin, *Poor Richard's Almanack* (Philadelphia: B. Franklin and D. Hall, 1758), spread 16, Rare Book Room/Octavo, http://www.rarebookroom.org/Control/frapoo/index.html (accessed April 14, 2010).

[7] Thomas Paine, *Common Sense* (Philadelphia: 1776), Gilder Lehrman Institute of American History, http://www.gilderlehrman.org/search/display_results.php?id=GLC03777 (accessed April 14, 2010).

[8] Bruce Chadwick, "Christmas, 1776: Private John Greenwood Crosses the Delaware, The War," in *The First American Army* (Naperville, Illinois: Sourcebooks, Inc., 2005), 140–41.

[9] George Washington's speech, quoted in Bruce Chadwick, "Christmas, 1776: Private John Greenwood Crosses the Delaware, The War," in *The First American Army*, 149–50.

[10] Mary Wollstonecraft, *A Vindication of the Rights of Woman: With Strictures on Moral and Political Subjects* (Philadelphia: William Gibbons, 1792), Rare Book and Special Collections Division, Library of Congress, http://www.loc.gov/rr/rarebook/digitalcoll/digitalcoll-american.html (accessed April 14, 2010).

[11] George Washington, "Farewell Address," *Connecticut Courant*, September 26, 1796, http://www.historybuff.com/archives/view.cgi/09-26-1796-1-f-tcc (accessed April 16, 2010).

[12] Gouverneur Morris, *The Diary and Letters of Gouverneur Morris* (New York: C. Scribner's Sons, 1888), 9, http://www.questia.com/PM.qst?a=o&d=9319145 (accessed April 16, 2010).

[13] Chadwick, *The First American Army*, 221.

[14] Supercomputing '94, "Thomas Jefferson," IEEE Computer Society and ACM SIGARCH, http://sc94.ameslab.gov/TOUR/tjefferson.html (accessed April 16, 2010).

[15] Thomas Jefferson, *The Writings of Thomas Jefferson,* vol. 9, (Washington, D.C.: issued under the Auspices of The Thomas Jefferson Memorial Association, 1907), 339–43, *Google Books,* http://books.google.com/books?id=MYJ2AAAAMAAJ& pg=PA18&lpg=PA18&dq=daniel+carroll+writings&sour ce=bl&ots=q1u6T0rNVq&sig=vROaHQmPJOoZerNAD AEs4kblR5Y&hl=en&ei=aHNnS- eHO86Wtge0u73jBg&sa=X&oi=book_result&ct=result &resnum=5&ved=0CBQQ6AEwBA#v=onepage&q=ind ependence&f=false (accessed April 16, 2010).

[16] Abraham Lincoln, *The Complete Works of Abraham Lincoln,* vol. 1 (1894; repr., New York: Francis D. Tandy Company, 1837), 43, http://lincoln.lib.niu.edu/cgi- bin/philologic/getobject.pl?c.124:1:0:0:11.lincoln (accessed April 16, 2010).

[17] Booker T. Washington, *An Autobiography: The Story of My Life and Work* (Chapel Hill: University of North Carolina, 1999), 315, http://docsouth.unc.edu/neh/washstory/washin.html (accessed April 16, 2010).

[18] *Letters of Members of the Continental Congress* vol. 1, ed. Edmund C. Burnett (Washington, D.C.: Carnegie Institution of Washington, 1921), *Google Books,* http://books.google.com/books?id=4AmKAAAAMAAJ

&printsec=frontcover&dq=Letters+of+Members+of+the
+Continental+Congress&source=bl&ots=I-
jWRQAAGe&sig=FFJA4vhPLJoShPtDGVb1NKbqFx8
&hl=en&ei=4fagS863EcWUtgeCoeDyBw&sa=X&oi=bo
ok_result&ct=result&resnum=2&ved=0CAwQ6AEwAQ
#v=onepage&q=&f=false (accessed April 16, 2010).

[19] John F. Kennedy, Inaugural Address, Washington, D.C.,
January 20, 1961.

[20] Thomas Jefferson, inscription at Jefferson Memorial,
Washington, D.C.

[21] Ashbrook Center for Public Affairs, "The Constitutional
Convention," Ashland University,
http://teachingamericanhistory.org/convention/ (accessed
April 17, 2010).

[22] Ashbrook Center for Public Affairs, James Madison,
*Notes of Debates in the Federal Convention of 1787*,
Ashland University,
http://teachingamericanhistory.org/convention/debates/05
28.html (accessed April 17, 2010).

[23] The following section describing constitutional theories
is largely based upon the author's notes taken during the
Constitutional Law lectures of Stephen H. Morris, J. D.,
of Freed-Hardeman University (author's private collection).

[24] William Woodson, "NJCOC Wednesday Evening Bible
Study," February 10, 2010,

http://www.northjacksonchurchofchrist.com/streaming_a
udio/2010/02-10-10_pm.mp3.

[25] Quoted in John Locke, *Two Treatises of Government*
(London: C. Baldwin, 1824), 162, *Google Books*,
http://books.google.com/books?id=K1UBAAAAYAAJ&
pg=PA162&lpg=PA162&dq=John+Locke+stated,+"Whe
re+there+is+no+law+there+is+no+freedom."&source=bl
&ots=jHQjiCik-Q&sig=4FPk-qYU-llwmPzF6g4AfA7-
vsc&hl=en&ei=3sfJS7LTEoLC9QS9r-
DMBA&sa=X&oi=book_result&ct=result&resnum=3&v
ed=0CAsQ6AEwAjgK#v=onepage&q=in%20all%20the
%20states%20of%20created%20beings%20capable%20o
f%20laws%2C%20%22where%20there%20is%20no%20
law%2C%20there%20is%20no%20freedom&f=false
(accessed April 17, 2010).

[26] Thomas Jefferson, inscription at Jefferson Memorial,
Washington, D.C.

[27] History has proven that many of the Anti-Federalists'
fears were not unfounded or ignorant. As indicated in
their writings (such as *The Anti-Federalist Papers*), the
Anti-Federalists had clearly studied for themselves the
proposed Constitution and were ready to protect themselves and their independence. See: *The Complete Anti-
Federalist*, ed. Herbert Storing (Chicago: University of
Chicago, 2007).

*Letters of Members of the Continental Congress* vol. 1, ed.
Edmund C. Burnett (Washington, D.C.: Carnegie Institution of Washington, 1921), *Google Books*,
http://books.google.com/books?id=4AmKAAAAMAAJ

&printsec=frontcover&dq=Letters+of+Members+of+the
+Continental+Congress&source=bl&ots=I-
jWRQAAGe&sig=FFJA4vhPLJoShPtDGVb1NKbqFx8
&hl=en&ei=4fagS863EcWUtgeCoeDyBw&sa=X&oi=bo
ok_result&ct=result&resnum=2&ved=0CAwQ6AEwAQ
#v=onepage&q=&f=false (accessed April 16, 2010).

[28] Alexander Hamilton, *Federalist No. 33*, *Daily Adver-
tiser*, January 3, 1788,
http://thomas.loc.gov/home/histdox/fed_33.html (accessed April 17, 2010).

[29] Ibid.

[30] James Madison, *Federalist No. 41*, *Independent Journal*,
http://thomas.loc.gov/home/histdox/fed_41.html (accessed April 17, 2010).

[31] "Welfare," *Merriam-Webster Online Dictionary*, 2010
http://www.merriam-webster.com/dictionary/welfare (accessed April 17, 2010).

[32] One might respond to this illustration by asserting that it
is misguided, given the illegal nature of the individuals'
pleasures. Yet, how is such any different than Congress
desiring to pass more and more restrictive and intrusive
laws—if those laws are in reality unconstitutional usurpa-
tions of power (illegal actions)?

[33] Marbury v. Madison, 5 U.S. 137 (1803).

[34] The remainder of the chapter is largely based upon the
author's notes taken during the Constitutional Law lec-

tures of Stephen H. Morris, J. D. (author's private collection).

[35] Gibbons v. Ogden, 22 U.S. 1 (1824).

[36] Brown v. Maryland, 25 U.S. 419 (1827).

[37] Schechter Poultry Corp. v. United States, 295 U.S. 495 (1935); and Carter v. Carter Coal Company, 298 U.S. 238 (1936).

[38] National Labor Relations Board v. Jones & Laughlin Steel Corporation, 301 U.S. 1 (1937).

[39] Wickard v. Filburn, 317 U.S. 111 (1942).

[40] John Locke, *Second Treatise* (New York: Mentor Books, New American Library, 1965), 94, quoted in *The Founder's Constitution*, vol. 1, chap. 17, doc. 5 (ed. Philip B. Kurland and Ralph Lerner), http://press-pubs.uchicago.edu/founders/documents/v1ch17s5.html (accessed April 17, 2010).

[41] Quote generally attributed to Hugo Black. See http://quotes.liberty-tree.ca/quotes_about/independence (accessed April 17, 2010).

[42] Thomas Jefferson, *The Writings of Thomas Jefferson*, quoted in Eyler Robert Coates, Sr., "Quotations from the Writings of Thomas Jefferson," part 4, http://religionanddemocracy.lib.virginia.edu/jefferson/quotations/jeff4.htm (accessed April 17, 2010).

[43] "Congressman: 'I Don't Worry About the Constitution' on Health Care Overhaul," FOX News, April 2, 2010, http://www.foxnews.com/politics/2010/04/02/democratic -lawmaker-dont-worry-constitution-health-care- overhaul/.

[44] John Locke, *The Works of John Locke, Esq.*, vol. 2 (London: Awnsham Churchill, 1722), 240, *Google Books*, http://books.google.com/books?id=pxjmAAAAMAAJ&p g=PA240&dq=John+Locke+The+Care+therefore+of+eve ry+man's+Soul+belongs+unto+himself,+and+is+to+be+l eft+unto+himself&hl=en&ei=- eHJS9vTNML38AaIqcHpBA&sa=X&oi=book_result&ct =result&resnum=2&ved=0CDgQ6AEwAQ#v=onepage& q=The%20Care%20therefore%20of%20every%20man's %20Soul%20belongs%20unto%20himself%2C%20and% 20is%20to%20be%20left%20unto%20himself&f=false (accessed April 17, 2010).

[45] Quote generally attributed to Pericles. See "Pericles," *Britannica Concise Encyclopedia*, http://www.answers.com/topic/pericles (accessed April 17, 2010).

[46] J. Caroline DeBerry, "The American Recovery and Re- investment Act of 2009: 'Bailing Out' on the Welfare of the American People" (paper for Contemporary Issues in American Public Policy, Freed-Hardeman University, June 20, 2009).

[47] "Economic Stimulus Program," http://obama-recovery- plan.com/economic-stimulus- pro-

gram/?fycid=4...0reinvestment%20act%20of%202009&g
clid=CK7c5c2-yjoCFQJ2xgodgym32g (accessed May 19,
2009).  See now:
http://change.gov/agenda/economy_agenda/ (accessed
June 16, 2010.

[48] Robert Schlesinger, "Lessons Barack Obama Can Learn
from FDR and the Hundred Days," *U.S. News & World
Report*, January 29, 2009,
http://www.usnews.com/articles/opinion/2009/01/29/less
ons-barack-obama-can-learn-from-fdr-and-the-hundred-
days_print.htm (accessed May 21, 2009).

[49] "Economic Stimulus Program."  See note 46 above.

[50] "Read the Stimulus," February 24, 2009,
http://www.readthestimulus.org/ (accessed May 19,
2009).

[51] Jason Chaffetz, "Statement of Congressman Jason Chaffetz Regarding American Recovery and Reinvestment
Act of 2009," February 13, 2009,
http://chaffetz.house.gov/2009/02/statement-of-
congressman-jason-chaffetz-regarding-american-
recovery-and-reinvestment-act-of-2009.shtml (accessed
May 21, 2009).

[52] "Overview of the American Recovery and Reinvestment
Act of 2009 (Recovery Act)," U.S. Small Business Ad-
ministration, http://www.sba.gov/recovery/ (accessed
May 19, 2009).

[53] Henry Ward Beecher, quoted in Robert E. Kelly, *The National Debt: From FDR (1941) to Clinton (1996)* (Jefferson, NC, and London: McFarland, 2000), introduction, *Google Books*, http://books.google.com/books?id=HmONpPZ_bugC&dq=the+national+debt+robert+kelly&printsec=frontcover&source=bl&ots=G8YS2qVk-O&sig=TltAdJ8HTVI2nzdDl4umkbO-j-k&hl=en&ei=ZvQ8SqblIoOytweRkYH9Dw&sa=X&oi=book_result&ct=result&resnum=1 (accessed May 21, 2009).

[54] Michael E. Kraft and Scott R. Furlong, *Public Policy: Politics, Analysis, and Alternatives* (Washington, D.C.: CQ Press, 2007), 191.

[55] Albert Einstein, "The Most Powerful Force in the Universe Is Compound Interest," Thinkexist.com, http://thinkexist.com/common/print.asp?id=158830&quote=the_most_powerful_force_in_the_universe_is (accessed June 18, 2009).

[56] "U.S. National Debt," iPhone Application, Readdle, January 15, 2009, Version 1.1 (accessed May 21, 2009).

[57] Ibid.

[58] Kraft and Furlong, *Public Policy*, 183.

[59] "H.R. 1: American Recovery and Reinvestment Act of 2009," *Congressional Budget Office Cost Estimate,* January 26, 2009, Congressional Budget Office,

http://www.cbo.gov/ftpdocs/99xx/doc9968/hr1.pdf (accessed May 19, 2009).

60 "Read the Stimulus," http://www.readthestimulus.org/.

61 Quoted in Paul Ryan, "True Cost of the So-Called 'Stimulus' Bill," TheJournalTimes.com, February 13, 2009, http://www.house.gov/ryan/speeches_and_editorials/2009 speechesandeditorials/21309RJTblog.htm (accessed January 21, 2009).

62 Benjamin Franklin, "Benjamin Franklin Quotes," WorldofQuotes.com, http://www.worldofquotes.com/author/Benjamin-Franklin/1/index.html (accessed May 21, 2009).

63 Ibid.

64 Lawrence H. White and David C. Rose, "We Can't Spend Our Way out of This Quagmire," *St. Louis Post-Dispatch*, January 21, 2009, http://www.cato.org/pub_display.php?pub_id=9901 (accessed May 19, 2009).

65 Benjamin Franklin, "Benjamin Franklin Quotes."

66 Alexander Hamilton, "Report on Public Credit," *The Debates and Proceedings of the Congress of the United States,* vol. 2 (December 13, 1790), 2042, http://memory.loc.gov/ll/llac/002/0300/03832041.tif (accessed May 21, 2009).

[67] Kraft and Furlong, *Public Policy*, 191.

[68] Similarly, two "porky" projects are likely to benefit from the Recovery Act—"parking improvements at a Little League facility in Cidra, Puerto Rico" ($150 million) and "'a snowmaking and maintenance facility' at Spirit Mountain ski area in Duluth, Minnesota" ($6 million). Matthew Bandyk, "Finding the Pork in the Obama Stimulus Bill," *U.S. News & World Report*, February 19, 2009, http://www.usnews.com/articles/business/economy/2009/02/19/finding-the-pork-in-the-obama-stimulus-bill.html (accessed May 19, 2009).

[69] Fred Lucas, "Stimulus Bill Raises Concerns Over Government Rationing of Health Care," CNSNews, February 11, 2009, http://www.cnsnews.com/public/content/article.aspx?RsrcID=43358 (accessed May 19, 2009).

[70] David A. Patten, "Obama's Bill Hands ACORN $5.2 Billion Bailout," *Newsmax*, January 27, 2009, http://www.newsmax.com/headlines/obama_bailout_bill/2009/01/27/175729.html (accessed May 19, 2009).

[71] Arnold Kling, "Deficit Spending: A Scenario Analysis," *Tax & Budget Bulletin*, February 2009, http://www.cato.org/pubs/tbb/tbb-54.pdf (accessed May 19, 2009). Of interest is one blogger's estimate that during only his first fifty days in office, Obama theoretically spent $530,092 per second. See: "Bush vs. Obama Total Budget Spent?" March 2009, Yahoo! Answers,

http://answers.yahoo.com/question/index?qid=200903232
31110AAXnTu2 (accessed May 21, 2009).

[72] Jason Chaffetz, "Statement of Congressman Jason Chaffetz."

[73] J. Bradford DeLong, *Slouching Towards Utopia?: The
Economic History of the Twentieth Century*, University of
California at Berkeley, February 3, 1997,
http://econ161.berkeley.edu/tceh/Slouch_Restoring11.ht
ml (accessed May 21, 2009).

[74] Ibid.

[75] Frank B. Tipton, *A History of Modern Germany Since
1815* (London: Continuum International Publishing
Group, 2003), 329–30, *Google Books,*
http://books.google.co.in/books?id=SQGMYLJRdXoC&
pg=PP1&dq=Frank+B+Tipton (accessed May 21, 2009).

[76] Harold Marcuse, "Historical Dollar-to-Marks Currency
Conversion Page" (last updated May 18, 2009), University of California at Santa Barbara,
http://www.history.ucsb.edu/faculty/marcuse/projects/cur
rency.htm (accessed May 21, 2009).

[77] "CPI Inflation Calculator," United States Department of
Labor, Bureau of Labor Statistics, http://data.bls.gov/cgi-
bin/cpicalc.pl (accessed May 22, 2009).

[78] On June 20, 2009, the CPI calculator indicated that $1 in
1921 would now have "the same buying power as $11.95
in 2009." Therefore, Germany's total reparations in to-

day's U.S. dollars would be approximately $27.48 billion. (Ibid.)

[79] John W. Schoen, "Just Who Owns the U.S. National Debt?" MSNBC.com, March 4, 2007, http://www.msnbc.msn.com/id/17424874/ns/business-personal_finance/page/2/print/1/displaymode/1098/ (accessed May 21, 2009).

[80] Anthony Faiola and Zachary A. Goldfarb, "China Tops Japan in U.S. Debt Holdings," *Washington Post*, November 19, 2008, http://www.washingtonpost.com/wp-dyn/content/article/2008/11/18/AR2008111803558.html (accessed May 21, 2009).

[81] Ambrose Evans-Pritchard, "Hillary Clinton Pleads with China to Buy US Treasuries as Japan Looks on," *Telegraph*, February 23, 2009, http://www.telegraph.co.uk/finance/financetopics/financialcrisis/4782755/Hillary-Clinton-pleads-with-China-to-buy-US-Treasuries-as-Japan-looks-on.html (accessed May 21, 2009).

[82] Hillary Clinton, quoted in Ambrose Evans-Pritchard, "Hillary Clinton Pleads with China to Buy US Treasuries as Japan Looks on," *Telegraph*, February 23, 2009, http://www.telegraph.co.uk/finance/financetopics/financialcrisis/4782755/Hillary-Clinton-pleads-with-China-to-buy-US-Treasuries-as-Japan-looks-on.html (accessed May 21, 2009).

[83] Similarly, on May 25, 2009, the Associated Press reported Secretary of the U.S. Treasury Timothy Geithner's

plans to visit China the following week, saying "he is expected to reassure Beijing about the strength of the U.S. dollar and thus the value of China's vast holdings of U.S. Treasury notes." See: Elaine Kurtenbach, "Speaker Pelosi Dodges Human Rights on China Visit," May 25, 2009, Associated Press, http://news.yahoo.com/s/ap/20090525/ap_on_re_as/as_ch ina_pelosi/print;_ylt=As71xYjGAqQds94pyHUhP.j9xg8 F;_ylu=X3oDMTB1MjgxN2UzBHBvcwMxNARzZWM DdG9vbHMtdG9wBHNsawNwcmludA-- (accessed May 25, 2009).

[84] Associated Press, "China Rejects Latest U.S. Report on Religious Freedom," *Anniston Star*, May 9, 2009, http://www.annistonstar.com/religion/2009/as-churchnews-0509-0-9e08u5520.htm (accessed May 21, 2009).

[85] Glenn Kessler and Michael D. Shear, "Human Rights Activists Troubled by Administration's Approach," *Washington Post*, May 5, 2009, http://www.washingtonpost.com/wp-dyn/content/article/2009/05/04/AR2009050403450_pf.ht ml (accessed May 21, 2009).

[86] Siobhan Gorman, "Electricity Grid in U.S. Penetrated by Spies," *Wall Street Journal*, April 8, 2009, http://online.wsj.com/article/SB123914805204099085.ht ml#printMode (accessed May 21, 2009).

[87] Ibid.

[88] Quoted in Schoen, "Just Who Owns the U.S. National Debt?"

[89] Proverbs 22:7. New King James Version.

[90] Patricia Rathbone, "When Good Fellows 'Give' Together," *Richmond Times Dispatch*, December 16, 1934, http://richmondthenandnow.com/Newspaper-Articles/Goodfellows-Christmas.html (accessed May 22, 2009).

[91] Kyle Wilkison, "The Great Depression and New Deal, 1929–1940s" and "Part II: War, Depression and War, 1914–1945," Collin County Community College, http://iws.ccccd.edu/kwilkison/Online1302home/20th%20Century/DepressionNewDeal.html (accessed May 21, 2009).

[92] N. Gregory Mankiw, "What Would Keynes Have Done?" *New York Times*, November 30, 2008, http://www.nytimes.com/2008/11/30/business/economy/30view.html?pagewanted=print (accessed May 22, 2009).

[93] "John Maynard Keynes—Theories," Biz/ed/Institute for Fiscal Studies (IFS) Virtual Library, http://www.bized.co.uk/virtual/economy/library/economists/keynesth.htm (accessed May 21, 2009).

[94] Quoted in Meg Sullivan, "FDR's Policies Prolonged Depression by 7 Years, UCLA Economists Calculate," *UCLA News*, August 10, 2004, http://newsroom.ucla.edu/portal/ucla/PRN-FDR-s-

Policies-Prolonged-Depression-5409.aspx (accessed May 21, 2009).

[95] Quoted in Steve Lohr, "F.D.R's Example Offers Lessons for Obama," *New York Times*, January 27, 2009, http://www.nytimes.com/2009/01/27/business/economy/27fdr.html?pagewanted=print (accessed May 22, 2009).

[96] Daniel J. Mitchell, "Spending Is Not Stimulus: Bigger Government Did Not Work for Bush, and It Will Not Work for Obama," *Tax & Budget Bulletin*, February 2009, http://www.cato.org/pubs/tbb/tbb_0209-53.pdf (accessed May 19, 2009).

[97] Jim Powell, "The 'Old' New Deal Still Isn't Paid for," *Forbes*, February 11, 2009, http://www.cato.org/pub_display.php/?pub_id=9971 (accessed May 22, 2009).

[98] "CPI Inflation Calculator," U.S. Department of Labor.

[99] "With All Due Respect Mr. President, That Is Not True," Cato Institute, http://www.cato.org/special/stimulus09/cato_stimulus.pdf (accessed May 22, 2009).

[100] Ibid.

[101] Ibid.

[102] Mitchell, "Spending is Not Stimulus."

[103] Amity Shlaes, "FDR Was a Great Leader, But His Economic Plan Isn't One to Follow," *Washington Post*, February 1, 2009, http://www.washingtonpost.com/wp-dyn/content/article/2009/01/30/AR2009013002760_pf.html (accessed May 22, 2009).

[104] Quoted in Ike Brannon and Chris Edwards, "The Troubling Return of Keynesianism," *Tax & Budget Bulletin*, January 2009, http://www.cato.org/pubs/tbb/tbb_0109-52.pdf (accessed May 19, 2009).

[105] Mankiw, "What Would Keynes Have Done?"

[106] "Bank Bailout Funds Mostly Spent," *Washington Times* March 29, 2009, http://www.washingtontimes.com/news/2009/mar/29/bank-bailout-fund-mostly-spent/print/ (accessed May 22, 2009).

[107] Deborah Solomon, David Enrich, and Jon Hilsenrath, "New Bank Bailout Could Cost $2 Trillion," *Wall Street Journal*, January 29, 2009, http://online.wsj.com/article/SB123319689681827391.html#printMode (accessed May 22, 2009).

[108] Sheryl Gay Stolberg, "Signing Stimulus, Obama Doesn't Rule Out More," *New York Times*, February 18, 2009, http://www.nytimes.com/2009/02/18/us/politics/18web-stim.html?pagewanted=print (accessed May 19, 2009).

[109] Seth Colter Walls and Peter Arkle, "What Can You Buy with Obama's 2010 Federal Budget?" *Newsweek*, May 25, 2009, 92.

[110] Barack Obama, quoted in Associated Press, "Obama Signs Stimulus into Law," MSNBC.com, February 17, 2009, http://www.msnbc.msn.com/id/29231790///print/1/displaymode/1098/ (accessed May 19, 2009).

[111] Shlaes, "FDR Was a Great Leader."

[112] Mankiw, "What Would Keynes Have Done?"

[113] "Senate Passes Reconciliation Health Bill," CBS/AP, March 25, 2010, http://www.cbsnews.com/stories/2010/03/25/politics/main6332715.shtml (accessed April 14, 2010).

[114] "U.S. National Debt," iPhone Application, Readdle, January 15, 2009, Version 1.1 (accessed March 31, 2010).

[115] James Pethokoukis, "China Questions Costs of U.S. Healthcare Reform," *Reuters*, November 16, 2009, http://blogs.reuters.com/james-pethokoukis/2009/11/16/china-questions-costs-of-us-healthcare-reform/.

[116] Jill Jackson and John Nolen, "Health Care Reform Bill Summary: A Look at What's in the Bill," CBSNews, March 21, 2010, http://www.cbsnews.com/8301-

503544_162-20000846-503544.html (accessed April 14, 2010).

[117] Douglas Holtz-Eakin, "The Real Arithmetic of Health Care Reform," *New York Times*, March 21, 2010, http://www.nytimes.com/2010/03/21/opinion/21holtz-eakin.html (accessed April 14, 2010).

[118] This book's author does not use the term "small businesses" to refer only to those with a certain number of employees; this author utilizes this term more generally, including any business the average citizen would consider "small." Yet, according to the CNN report (by deMause), the health care reform legislation applies the following standard: "small businesses" are defined as those with no more than 100 employees, though states have the option of limiting pools to companies with 50 or fewer employees through 2016; companies that grow beyond the size limit will also be grandfathered in."
Neil deMause, "What Health Care Reform Means for Your Business," CNNMoney.com, March 22, 2010, http://money.cnn.com/2010/03/22/smallbusiness/small_business_health_reform/index.htm (accessed April 14, 2010).

[119] Quoted in Aldo Svaldi, "Small-business Owners Uncertain about Health Bill's Effects," *Denver Post*, March 23, 2010, http://www.denverpost.com/business/ci_14735516 (accessed April 14, 2010).

[120] Pat Wechsler, "Doctors Get Reprieve from 21% Medicare Payment Cut (Update 1)," *BusinessWeek*, March 29, 2010, http://www.businessweek.com/news/2010-03-

29/doctors-get-reprieve-from-21-decline-in-payments-from-medicare.html (accessed April 14, 2010).

[121] Robert Lowes, "Organized Medicine Blasts Congress for Failing to Stop Medicare Pay Cut," Medscape Medical News, May 28, 2010, http://www.medscape.com/viewarticle/722694 (accessed May 29, 2010).

[122] John W. House, "21% Cut to Medicare Will Create Two-Tier Health Care System," *Huffington Post*, April 14, 2010, http://www.huffingtonpost.com/john-w-house-md/21-cut-to-medicare-will-c_b_493774.html (accessed April 14, 2010).

[123] Mark Sklar, "A Doctor's Reflections on Health-Care Reform," *Wall Street Journal*, June 23, 2009, http://online.wsj.com/article/SB124571387059539071.html (accessed April 14, 2010).

[124] House, "21% Cut to Medicare."

[125] Sklar, "A Doctor's Reflections."

[126] Donna Smith, comment on "Q+A: How Does Healthcare Overhaul Affect Medicare?" *Reuters*, March 22, 2010, http://www.reuters.com/article/idUSTRE62J1FS20100322 (accessed March 31, 2010).

[127] Quoted in "Federal Legislative Activities on Medicare," American Medical Association, http://www.ama-assn.org/ama/pub/advocacy/current-topics-

advocacy/practice-management/medicare-physician-payment-reform-regulatory-relief/federal-legislative-activities-medicare.shtml (accessed June 5, 2010).

128 "Health Care," and "Health Reform," White House, http://www.whitehouse.gov/Issues/health-Care (accessed March 31, 2010).

129 J. Caroline DeBerry, "A Must for Minorities: Support of Republicans—the True Thwarters of Poverty" (paper for Diversity in America, Freed-Hardeman University, April 29, 2008).

130 Bill Frist, *A Heart to Serve: The Passion to Bring Health, Hope, and Healing* (New York: Center Street, 2009), 331, http://www.BillFrist.com/assets/HealthPolicyGeneral.pdf (accessed June 16, 2010).

131 Jamie Ward, "Exclusive Interview with Congressman and M.D. Tom Price of Georgia's 6th District," *Atlanta Citizen*, March 22, 2010, http://theatlantacitizen.com/exclusive-interview-with-congressman-and-m-d-tom-price-of-georgias-6th-district (accessed April 14, 2010).

132 Ibid.

133 Ralph Goodman, MD, e-mail interview by author, April 4, 2010.

134 Ward, "Exclusive Interview."

[135] *Letters of Members of the Continental Congress* vol. 1, ed. Edmund C. Burnett (Washington, D.C.: Carnegie Institution of Washington, 1921), 58, *Google Books*, http://books.google.com/books?id=4AmKAAAAMAAJ &printsec=frontcover&dq=Letters+of+Members+of+the +Continental+Congress&source=bl&ots=I-jWRQAAGe&sig=FFJA4vhPLJoShPtDGVb1NKbqFx8 &hl=en&ei=4fagS863EcWUtgeCoeDyBw&sa=X&oi=bo ok_result&ct=result&resnum=2&ved=0CAwQ6AEwAQ #v=onepage&q=&f=false (accessed April 16, 2010).

[136] "Louis D. Brandeis Quotes" and "Justice Louis D. Brandeis," Louis D. Brandeis Legacy Fund for Social Justice, http://www.brandeis.edu/legacyfund/bio.html (accessed April 19, 2010).

[137] Ken Millstone, "A Tie—Down To The Vote—In N.Y. House Race," CBS News, April 4, 2009, http://www.cbsnews.com/8301-503544_162-4919528-503544.html?tag=contentMain;contentBody (accessed April 14, 2010).

[138] "Cigarette Smoking" and "Prevention and Early Detection," American Cancer Society, http://www.cancer.org/docroot/PED/content/PED_10_2X _Cigarette_Smoking_and_Cancer.asp (accessed April 14, 2010).

[139] Mary Branham Dusenberry, "Butts Out: Many States Now Ban Smoking in Public Places," *State News* 18 (August 2007), http://www.csg.org/knowledgecenter/docs/sn0708ButtsO ut.pdf (accessed June 3, 2010).

140 Steven Reinberg, "Report: Nationwide Smoking Ban Would Reduce Heart Attacks," USATODAY.com, May 21, 2010, http://www.usatoday.com/news/health/2010-05-21-smoking-ban_N.htm (accessed April 14, 2010).

141 Quote generally attributed to John Quincy Adams. See http://quotes.liberty-tree.ca/quotes_about/independence (accessed April 14, 2010).

142 Marjorie Crayton, telephone interview by author, April 5, 2010.

143 Fred and Pat Allen, e-mail interview by author, March 20, 2010.

144 Whitney v. California, 274 U.S. 357, 375-77 (1927).

145 Quote generally attributed to Samuel Adams. See http://quotes.liberty-tree.ca/quote_blog/Samuel.Adams.Quote.CEB3 (accessed June 16, 2010).

146 Dan Reiter and Allan C. Stam, *Democracies at War* (Princeton: Princeton University Press, 2002), 62, *Google Books*, http://books.google.com/books?id=8yzs3V8EXXwC&printsec=frontcover&dq=Democracies+at+war+by+dan+reiter&hl=en&ei=ALbNS9LqJY3a9AS11Yy0Dw&sa=X&oi=book_result&ct=result&resnum=1&ved=0CDkQ6AEwAA#v=onepage&q=Individual%20liberty&f=false (accessed April 20, 2010).

147 Ward, "Exclusive Interview."

[148] Jamie Ward, "Exclusive Interview With Congressman and M.D. Tom Price of Georgia's 6th District," *Atlanta Citizen*, March 22, 2010, http://theatlantacitizen.com/wp-content/uploads/2010/03/Congressman-Tom-Price-MD-Question3answer-2010_03_22_02_01.mp3 (accessed April 14, 2010).

# MORE ABOUT THE AUTHOR...

From other correspondence about or sent to
Caroline DeBerry:

"Caroline consistently demonstrated a diligent work ethic
and dedication to having an impact in the political process
and public service." ~ **Governor Sonny Perdue** (2005)

"Much of our success is directly due to your great work!"
~ **U.S. Congressman Tom Price** (2008)